The Greaseless Guide to Car Care Confidence

The Greaseless Guide to Car Care Confidence

Take the Terror Out of Talking to Your Mechanic

Mary Jackson

John Muir Publications

Santa Fe, New Mexico

John Muir Publications, P.O. Box 613, Santa Fe, NM 87504
© 1989 by Mary Jackson
Cover and illustrations © 1989 by John Muir Publications
Printed in the United States of America

First edition. Fifth printing July 1993

Library of Congress Cataloging-in-Publication Data

Jackson, Mary, 1946-
  The greaseless guide to car care confidence: take the terror
out of talking to your mechanic/Mary Jackson. — 1st ed.
      p. cm.
  Includes index.
  ISBN 0-945465-19-X
  1. Automobiles—Maintenance and repair—Amateurs'
manuals.
I. Title.
TL152.J275 1989   89-9290
629.28'722—dc20   CIP

Illustrations: Jim Finnell
Typeface: Century Schoolbook
Typesetter: Copygraphics, Santa Fe
Text designer: Joanna V. Hill

Printed on Recycled Paper by Banta Company

Distributed to the book trade by:
W. W. Norton & Company, Inc.
New York, New York

Contents

Preface

Garage-ese is a language developed and spoken by motor-tech-heads to other motor-tech-heads. Unfortunately, it is also spoken to non-motor-tech-heads. This book has been written to close the gap between the two. It is exclusively for those who may never tune or troubleshoot but who, nevertheless, would like to be able to speak confidently, to understand, and to be clearly understood when it comes to buying a car or having their car repaired.

As the only girl growing up in a family of five boys, I did not learn garagese at home. Information about cars was placed on a "need to know" basis, and in our family, girls did not need to know.

That worked fine until I began driving my own car. I quickly discovered that I had a definite need to know. I had a need to know about new sounds coming from my car. Did they mean a $2 or a $200 repair? Or should I begin looking for a new car? I had a need to know about routine maintenance. Was I doing the right thing by checking the engine oil every leap year? I had a need to know about repairs and pricing. Was I being treated fairly, or did mechanics identify my obvious ignorance as fair game? Having almost no knowledge of my car and no language with which to learn about it, I struggled hopelessly with repair explanations and in the end, reluctantly and blindly delegated full responsibility to mechanics.

My vulnerability, frustration, and sense of powerlessness ended when I moved to a small Vermont town and, in an effort to avoid starvation, took a job in a local body shop.

There, among the tack rags and paint fumes, while doing general repair work, I had my first opportunity to look inside cars. Engines, transmissions, and brakes began to make sense as I peeled back the outside and observed their basic parts and relationships. All the while, like a three-year-old, asking hundreds of "why questions."

This book is intended to pass on my learning experience, sans paint fumes, with the hope that knowing the basics about cars will help you to open the door to understanding them as it has done for me. It is not an exhaustive work but rather a framework for building car care confidence and providing protection from car repair ripoff.

I would like to thank Dan Donza for opening up the world of cars to me and for helping me in too many ways to mention to make this book possible; Lenny Bisceglia for his knowledge, time, patience, and unique explanations of how cars tick; the following Stowe, Vermont, repair shops: Mt. Mansfield Garage, David's Shell, Bucky's Repair, and Willy's Village Auto, all of whom contributed in some way to my assembling this information. I also want to thank Charles "Fritz" Halstead, master mechanic at Boulder Toyota, the staff at Nickerson Sinclair in Boulder, Colorado, and the many fine mechanics throughout this country who have provided me with technical information. Thanks also go to the participants who have attended my workshops. Their intelligent questions and insightful comments have been an invaluable help.

I am very fortunate to have as my publisher John Muir Publications. Jim Finnell's illustrations have made the words come alive as I had always hoped they would, with clarity and humor. Speaking of words, I owe much to editor Barbara Daniels, who patiently helped me find the right ones.

I want to thank my friends for propping me up when this project looked bigger than a house and celebrating with me when it began to look more like a finished work. There is Michele Patenaude, editor of *Vermont Woman Magazine*, who contributed in every imaginable way to helping me write this book but especially for convincing me that I could write it. There is also my family, both Horans and Marshalls, whose nonstop encouragement made a huge difference. A special thanks to Patricia

Marshall and Janet Savage for their contribution to the title and to Jim Marshall, who through it all steadfastly helped me keep things in perspective.

And finally there are my parents, the late Leonard F. and C. Patricia Horan, who taught me that there is no knowledge that is either inappropriate or unattainable.

Introduction

Your car has been making weird noises, so you bring it to a garage to be fixed. Later you arrive to pick it up and the mechanic hands you a bill that's completely illegible, except for the $275 total. You don't know what to do.

You're running a few minutes late for an important interview. You jump in your car, turn the key, and nothing happens. You don't know what to do.

You're driving down a lonely highway and you get a flat tire. There's not another car in sight. You don't know what to do.

Powerlessness. It's a familiar feeling and one you might experience in dealing with the everyday problems of owning and driving a car. Consider the importance of the automobile in our lives. Most of us depend on our cars every day. They are essential to holding down jobs and running our busy lives. A car is likely to be the second largest item in our budget; the largest, if we don't have a mortgage.

Yet what really goes on under the hood of your car may be as mysterious as the Transporter on the Starship Enterprise. Why is it so mysterious? Is it understandable only to those with special knowledge and powers of perception? Can only a select few learn its hidden secrets? Of course not.

Car Mystique

Most of us didn't get together with our pals to give the old Chevy a tune-up, unless we grew up in a family where

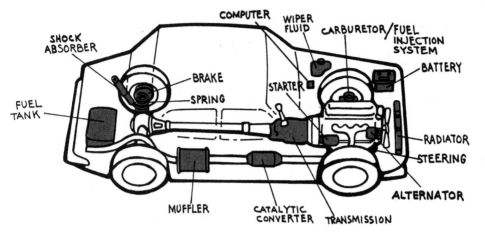

some member was a backyard mechanic. If we were not shown the differences between the V-8 and the slant 6, we just didn't get to learn how cars ticked.

For many years, our ignorance didn't really seem to matter. During the 1950s and 1960s, a few giant-sized domestic manufacturers sold us cars while local service stations, manned by mechanics we knew and who knew us, fixed most things that went wrong. There was some degree of accountability, or so we hoped.

By the 1970s, the oil embargos were whittling away at the number of independent service stations. In their place appeared sterile self-serve replacements selling everything from microwave burritos to baseball cards—but not service. Government agencies were beginning to control our car's harmful pollutants. Auto manufacturers responded with smaller and smaller cars that ran on more fuel-efficient engines that produced fewer emissions. As more and more cars jammed the overburdened highways, however, traditional methods of burning fuel were not enough.

From the halls of high technology came the computer. Electronic brains in the form of little "black boxes" replaced traditional mechanical parts. Their lightning fast accuracy burned fuel more efficiently, thus eliminating even more pollutants while improving the power and performance that had initially been sacrificed for economic and environmental concerns. With complex computers came complex diagnosis and repair. Our automotive lives would never be the same.

Small shops very often could not afford the costly diagnostic equipment and Manhattan telephone book-sized manuals, without which the newer cars were unfathomable. Nor could they keep pace with the constant influx of technical information. Car dealerships, which only work on the cars they sell, large franchises, and automotive specialists that only fix certain types of cars (usually imported), all armed with expensive diagnostic equipment, replaced many of the independents that had been the backbone of the repair industry.

Our ignorance of the car was beginning to take on a new and different significance. The repair person who had known our car intimately and knew when we said "shimmy" we really meant "vibrate," who knew when we scrinched up our faces funny and made a sound like a crazed bumble bee that the speedometer cable needed lubrication, who every time our car was on a lift knew to inspect it thoroughly to discover any hidden problems we weren't expected to know about was gone. Often we never saw the person who worked on our cars, or had the opportunity to tell the mechanic what was wrong.

Speaking Garage-ese

We now had to talk to intermediaries. "Garage-ese" (car lingo), which had never seemed very important, became increasingly frustrating to understand and speak. We were like tourists visiting a foreign country with no knowledge of the language, no understanding of the currency exchange rate, and no map. On arriving in the capital city, we ask a taxi driver to take us to a nearby ruin. The trip seems to take forever. Did we cross another border on the way? We finally arrive, hand the cabby a fistful of the local currency, close our eyes, and hope that we aren't going to be taken for another kind of ride.

As our cars have become more complex, we have become increasingly likely to blindly delegate responsibility for our cars to strangers, hoping that we won't be taken advantage of, at least not too much. Sometimes putting all the responsibility for our welfare in the hands of strangers works. Sometimes it doesn't. It backfires when repairs are diagnosed incorrectly, are not done right the first time, are done when unnecessary, or are done appropriately but at an outrageous cost. When it comes to our cars, the real issues are not so much mechanical as financial.

It's not that car dealers and mechanics are involved in some plot to take advantage of us. It's just that in every field, there are the good, the bad, and the indifferent. If we don't have a basic understanding of how our cars work and the command of a few principles of autologic, we are unable to tell the difference.

What a different trip it might have been had we arrived with a pocket dictionary of important phrases, a calculator with which to compute the exchange rate, and a map of the city. We might not have known that the cabby had taken us a few blocks out of the way to make a few more dollars, but we would have known if he had decided to circle the entire town before dropping us at our destination. And we would have known if the fare was reasonable given what we knew about the exchange rate. This book is the equivalent of a pocket dictionary, a calculator, and a map of the city.

Cars are too complex for a book this size to make us fluent in the native language. The car has an average of 15,000 parts, 1,500 of which move. Add to this an on-board computer or two and throw in a dozen or more emission control components, whose job it is to reduce pollutants, most of which can create problems that show up as symptoms that look and act like the more traditional parts and systems did.

Fortunately, we're in luck—cars are logical and systematic. And just as with all systems, if you begin with the basics, they can be broken down into bite-size pieces and eventually understood.

Cars and Bicycles

A car works something like a bicycle. When the bicyclist pedals, she generates up and down power through her legs. That power makes both the bicycle chain and the wheels

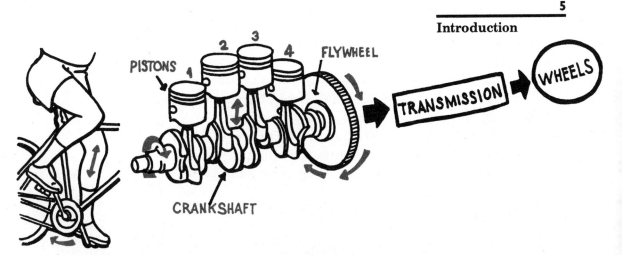

turn. Up and down power is converted into rotational power. And down the road the bicycle goes.

Inside each car's engine there are three or more round metal plugs called pistons, which are attached to a round metal bar called the crankshaft. Like the bicyclist's legs, these pistons move up and down. Their up and down power turns the crankshaft, which, through the transmission, turns the car's wheels. Once again, up and down power is converted into rotational power, and down the road you go.

Just as the bicyclist needs a balanced diet to perform well at generating power, so does your car's engine. Instead of green vegetables, Grape Nuts, and granola bars, a car wants air (the kind we all breathe), fuel (gasoline), and fire (a hot spark). When these three elements are compressed and combined in the hollow tubes (cylinders) that house the pistons, at the right proportions at the right time, it's like dropping a match into a container of gasoline. Boom! The air/fuel mixture explodes and expands, releasing its energy, which pushes the pistons away. And because they are attached to the crankshaft, they move rapidly up and down. Their movement causes the crankshaft to spin.

Just as the chemical energy of the bicyclist's body is converted into the mechanical energy of the bicycle's wheels, so is the chemical energy of the exploding gases converted into the mechanical energy of the moving pistons, crankshaft, and eventually the car's wheels. If the bicyclist's diet is unbalanced, for example, if she forgets her green vegetables or eats too much sugar and not enough carbohydrates, eventually she begins to feel unwell. Inevitably, her bicycling performance suffers. She just doesn't have the get up and go to generate the power that she did when her diet was correctly balanced. Hills that were once a piece of cake now look like Pike's Peak.

Cars also suffer if their diet is unbalanced. Too much air, too much fuel, or a spark that is not hot enough or delivered at the wrong time will result in poor performance. Hard starting, lack of acceleration, stalling, surging, hesitating, and low gas mileage are all symptoms that may be related to an unbalanced diet.

The Proper Care and Feeding of Your Car

Preventive maintenance is linked to a proper diet. Your car can't go out and buy what it needs to take of itself. It needs you to do that by periodically scheduling routine maintenance, or service as it is now called. Just as you routinely visit your dentist to have your teeth examined, cleaned, and repaired when necessary, and to have minor adjustments made in your bite so that things work optimally, so should you schedule service for your car. It takes a professional who knows how to perform a precise series of tests and adjustments to keep the correct proportions and timing of the air-fuel-fire diet so that your car runs smoothly. Furthermore, parts must be repaired or replaced as they wear or break.

In addition, routine maintenance fights two enemies that arouse dread in the heart of every car: dirt (the garden variety) and heat (enough is generated by your car's engine to melt ordinary steel). They would send your car to an early grave after a lifetime of expensive repairs and the replacement of major parts if correct preventive maintenance were not performed on time.

Just as people are equipped with filters to keep their systems free of contaminants (liver, kidneys, and so on), so also are cars. Air, oil, and fuel are just a few of the many filters that keep the dust and dirt naturally present in the atmosphere from invading and damaging the finely machined parts of your car's engine and its other systems. In order for them to continue to perform effectively, they must be replaced at regular intervals.

Dirt and foreign particles can also clog the tiny openings or passageways that carry essential fluids for the lubrication of places where two metal parts rub together. Cars and people need fluids to survive. Without oil (engine and transmission), coolant, brake fluid, power steering, and other fluids, your car wouldn't last any longer than you would without an adequate supply of blood and water. Automotive fluids, which are circulated through hoses driven by pumps, perform many jobs, including holding contaminants in suspension, lubricating and reducing friction, and controlling the offspring of friction—heat.

Because cars are idiosyncratic, there is no one right maintenance schedule for all cars. The appropriate schedule for your car is found in your owner's manual. There you will find two categories, severe and normal service. Read the description of each category carefully to decide under which conditions you usually drive your car. By keeping your car on its service schedule, you spend a limited amount of money every year in order to avoid spending unlimited amounts of money later on the repair or replacement of prematurely worn parts.

About your owner's manual—most of you probably have yours sitting by the bedside table, within easy reach, so that you can go over and over those particularly fun-filled pages. You know, the dog-eared ones? What? You haven't read it? You don't even know what it looks like? You do know what it looks like, but you've only read it once to find the defroster knob in a blinding snowstorm?

Nobody can blame you. Next to insurance policies, owners' manuals make for some of the dullest reading imaginable. That fact notwithstanding, they contain extremely important information about your car, information that is seldom available anywhere else outside of textbook-sized repair manuals. Furthermore, it is probably the only free information you're likely to get which explains your car to you. Sundry little facts such as whether your car can be pushed, pulled, or towed without doing damage to it can often be found only in the manual. If it happens that your car gets pushed, pulled, or towed when it's not supposed to be pushed, pulled, or towed, you will wish you had put that little book on your reading list.

Your owner's manual also has information such as the specific requirements for replacement fluids. Put in the wrong weight oil, for example, 10W 30 instead of the manual's recommended 10W 40, and the warranty may be voided if a problem with the engine develops which can be related to oil. The result may be embarrassment and unnecessary expense. Furthermore, a fluid that is good for one car is not necessarily good for another. What your neighbor's car wants may be entirely different from what yours requires, that is, unless you both have the same make, model, and year. In that case, you can opt for the true pinnacle of owner's manual intimacies—you can read it together.

So put down that best seller and add a brand new dimension to your reading. And when you're done, put your manual in the glove compartment where it's handy. It's a valuable source of information and a vital key to the reduction of your car care vulnerability.

Car Care Confidence

It's time to reevaluate the system. You may not want to change your own oil or replace an air filter, or attend votech school, and you don't have to. There are honest and competent professionals ready and willing to work on your car. This book will help you to learn to recognize them— and to deal with them when you find them.

Finding a good mechanic is essential, but it is not enough to ensure good car care. Even the best mechanics are not magicians or psychics or even private detectives.

You can't expect to drive in with your ailing auto, say "It's broken," and have your mechanic know exactly what's wrong, then fix it immediately for a reasonable price. Before your mechanic can diagnose or fix the problem, he or she needs to know what symptoms have brought you and your car to the garage.

Understanding how your car works will help you when talking with a mechanic. Reading your owner's manual and learning the basics about how cars work are good strategies to protect yourself from unneeded, phoney, or overpriced repairs. Once you understand how the basic systems work, you can use everyday language to communicate with your mechanic as long as you are clear, accurate, and thorough in describing your car's symptoms. When you know what a fuel injector is and does, you will be better able to discuss its problem and how to solve it. You will also be better able to understand the explanations of what was found and what was done. Knowledge is your protection. It is how you can empower yourself.

To begin, take the idea that cars are mystical and throw it out the nearest window. And with it, toss the argument that computers have made cars too complex to be explained or understood by anyone other than technicians. A computer in your car operates as a computer does in the rest of your life: data in, data out. Computers have taken over specific jobs that were traditionally done by mechanical components. If you understand the traditional job, for example, ignition, then you can make the leap to a computerized ignition. It's simply one more layer to digest mentally and understand.

Shifting from the passenger to the driver's seat when it comes to car care depends on accessing meaningful information. If the person with whom you communicate about service for your car—service writer, technician, mechanic—thoroughly understands how your car works (and why at times it doesn't), and has the skill and the intention to translate the technical terms into English, you are far more likely to have a satisfactory relationship with your car. Whomever you choose to service your car, base your choice not only on their technical competence but also on their ability to effectively communicate technical information to you.

Use this book to unlock your car's logical secrets; they are yours for the asking. Knowing about cars is a right, but rights have to be exercised. It's not always going to be comfortable to assert those rights, especially in the beginning. But just in the act of deciding to take charge of your car, a personal and empowering change will take place. A flat tire on a lonely road—once a horrible nightmare—will instead become only an inconvenience. Now you do know what to do.

2

Carburetors and Fuel Injectors: The Diet, Parts 1 and 2

Carburetion

"Carburetor" was just one of the "secret" words that was thrown knowingly around by my brothers as they poked their heads under the hoods of the cars parked in front of our home. As a kid growing up, I placed such words in the UNKNOWN category. For me, that meant not only unknown but UNKNOWABLE. It was as if there was a secret club, and I was not a member. When I finally learned what a carburetor really was and did, I also discovered there was no secret club.

CARBURETOR

It is the carburetor—or its modern computerized cousin, the fuel injection system—that combines the first two parts of the engine's diet: air and fuel, the topics of this chapter. We'll look at the third part of the diet, fire, in chapter 3.

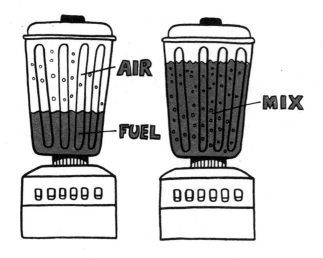

The carburetor is actually the food blender of your car's engine. The carburetor draws measured amounts of air from outside the car and combines it, in a very special way, with measured amounts of gasoline drawn from a tank in the rear of the car (as far away from the engine's spark as possible). This mixture is then distributed to the cylinders, the heart of the engine.

In the carburetor, the liquid gasoline is transformed into a a fine spray or mist, similar to that from a hair spray bottle or a cologne atomizer. By making its molecules smaller, the carburetor has turned the gasoline into a vapor or a fume.

Vaporized gas, which burns much easier than gasoline in its liquid form, is exactly what the doctor ordered. When this gasoline burns, its heated gases expand, pushing the pistons—the real shakers and movers of this show—away, and causing them to move up and down. This action is the foundation for the "combustion" in the internal combustion engine.

Air Filter

Cars require an enormous amount of air to breathe; about 9,000 gallons of air are needed for every one gallon of gasoline. By anyone's reckoning, that's a lot. It is important for the smooth running and long life of your car that the air it breathes is clean, that is, free of dirt and dust. It is

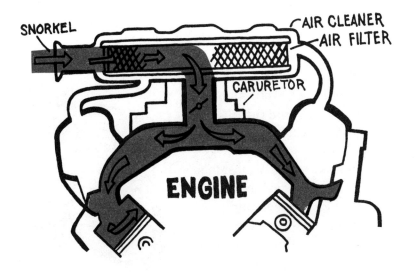

the job of the appropriately named "air cleaner" to do just that.

A breather hose, commonly called a snorkel, actually carries the air from outside the car into the carburetor. En route, it is heated by hot air redirected from the engine. The air passes through the air cleaner, a metal or plastic container, that houses the air filter—the workhorse of this cleanup detail. The filter, made of pleated folds of paper, catches plain old garden variety airborne dust and dirt before it gets down into the tiny openings, or passageways, of the carburetor.

If the dirt reaches any of these openings, it can block the passage of air and gasoline, unbalancing the diet; however, if the dirt moves through the openings, the consequences may be even more serious. Lodged between the finely machined moving metal parts of the engine located below the carburetor, the dirt is a constant irritant. Like a piece of sand in an oyster shell, the dirt scratches the smooth surfaces of the engine's internal parts, causing them to wear prematurely. Unlike the oyster, you won't get a pearl, but you can count on a gem of a repair bill.

The air filter works like any home furnace filter. It traps dirt and dust and must be changed when it's full. Most cars need a new filter about once a year, every 12,000 miles, or whenever your owner's manual recommends. If you happen to live in the Sahara, next to the Great Salt

Lake, or merely on an extremely dusty road, you will probably want to decrease the time between changes.

For years the air filter could be easily found under the hood. Checking and changing the filter was the classic do-it-yourself chore. Anyone who wanted to could save a few dollars by removing a wing nut and a couple of clamps and performing a simple test. You would just hold the filter up to a light: if light could be seen coming through one side, the filter was still in good shape.

But wait. Something simple? Easy to do? Almost foolproof? Look out! Today the air cleaner is disguised in a wide range of sizes, shapes, and colors. Some manufacturers now advise that it should only be removed by a trained professional. They warn that the flow of air to the engine may be interrupted if, when the filter is replaced, it is positioned incorrectly. If the airflow is interrupted, the car may run roughly or not at all. A few dollars savings may turn into ten times that spent on a visit to the repair shop to correct the problem.

There are other reasons it may be easier, and wiser, to have your mechanic decide when the air filter needs changing. On some recent models, the filter may be gray or black when new, making it impossible to tell when it needs changing. The principle behind this, I'm told, is that many of us can't tell when a filter is dirty or clean. Ay-yi-yi! If Do-It-Yourself isn't dead, it sure is breathing hard!

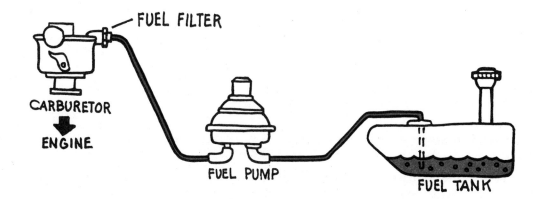

FUEL FILTER

CARBURETOR

ENGINE

FUEL PUMP

FUEL TANK

Fuel Pump and Fuel Filter

To get the gasoline from the rear of the car, a fuel pump
(sometimes more than one), located either in the gas tank
or between the tank and the engine, pushes the gasoline
along the fuel lines, which lie along the bottom of the car.
Until the 1970s, fuel pumps were mechanically driven by
an attachment to the turning engine. The majority of cars
being manufactured today use pumps that are driven electrically. Problems with an electric fuel pump should begin
with a check of the simple and inexpensive fuse that
ensures its proper functioning. Within the tank, there is
also a device called a sending unit that monitors the
amount of gasoline and sends that information in the form
of electronic impulses, which are registered by the needle
on a gas gauge located on the dashboard. In chapter 7,
we'll talk more about sending units and electricity in
general.

On its way to the carburetor or fuel injectors, the gasoline passes through one or more fuel filters, miniature versions of the air filter, which catch dirt and foreign particles
before they reach the working parts of the carburetor or
fuel injectors. The clean gas then reaches the carburetor or
injectors where it mixes with the air.

A fuel filter may be small, but it's mighty. This tiny filter is responsible for cleaning all the gasoline that passes
through it, a task it can perform only if changed regularly.
The fuel filter in most cars should be changed about once a
year, every 10,000 miles, or whenever your owner's manual says.

At this point, it appears that the carburetor is a pretty
simple device. (You know better though, don't you?) What

increases its complexity are the constantly changing demands of your car's engine for different proportions of air and gas at different times. While an engine may want only a ratio a of 14:1 (14 parts of air for every 1 of gasoline) when it's sitting at a stop sign, it may demand a 18:1 ratio when passing another car.

Even the simplest carburetor has many moving parts that must be adjusted properly and able to move freely. If any of these parts is worn, broken, or frozen, there is no way that a correct mixture of air and gasoline will result. Sometimes turning a single carburetor adjustment screw ¼ inch to the left or right will solve the problem of a rough running or stalling engine. Replacement of the worn out or broken part with a "kit" may solve the problem. Sometimes, however, the whole carburetor needs to be replaced.

If replacement is suggested, be sure to ask if a "rebuilt" carburetor is available. New carburetors, the computer-assisted models called "feed-back carburetors," can cost plenty just for the part! A savings of as much as 40 percent off the price of a new one is well worth considering. The rebuilt part has usually had the internal parts removed, examined, and replaced, when necessary, with new ones. The shell, which normally sees little wear, is used again. Rebuilts may take longer to get, however, so think carefully before saying yes to this alternative. If you do go for a rebuilt, be sure it is factory rebuilt, and says so, or has a minimum 60-day written warranty from the company that did the rebuild.

The Choke

Ever wonder why a car that starts just fine all summer long gets finicky when the weather turns cold? It all has to do with the way gasoline responds to cold temperatures. Instead of mixing freely with the air to form a fine mist, gasoline gets heavier when it's cold and turns into larger droplets that condense on the inside of the carburetor walls. This condensation causes the diet to be short on fuel. To compensate, a door, called a choke plate, is located on top of the carburetor. This door closes when it's cold, reducing the amount of air and forcing more gasoline into the mixture. This "richer" mixture (more gasoline than normal) helps to compensate for the effects of cold temperatures. As the engine warms, its heat causes the choke plate to open gradually, allowing the mixture to return to a normal, more fuel-efficient proportion.

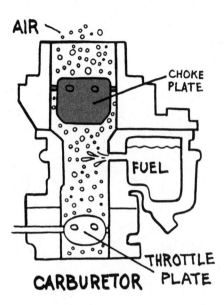

The chokes on most newer cars operate automatically, but on older cars, the opening and closing is done by manually by pulling a knob marked "Choke" on the dash. The choke is pulled out, forcing the choke plate to remain in a closed position until the engine warms up. It is then pushed in so that the choke plate can open further. If the choke is malfunctioning, you may find on cold days that the engine will be hard to start or won't start at all.

Fuel Injection

Since the 1970s, the demand for cars to burn less gasoline, generate less pollution, and still go fast has increased. In response, carburetors have grown bigger and bigger. Eventually, all kinds of hoses and wires were found hanging off them. The more complicated and more expensive they became, the more difficult they were to fix when things went wrong. And still the demands increased.

The solution came in the form of fuel injection—the

modern-day equivalent of the carburetor. About 95 percent of the cars being built today are equipped with this
more modern blender, which does the same job as a carburetor but mixes faster and more efficiently, resulting in
reduced pollution. Good news for everyone! It also provides
more power, while permitting the engine to run on a
"leaner" mixture, in other words, less fuel used in proportion to air. Who could ask for anything more?

There are two types of computerized fuel injection:
throttle body and multi-port. Throttle body fuel injection
is not much more than a souped-up carburetor and looks
like one that is missing its insides. It sprays a common
measure of the air/fuel mixture down to the engine below,
where the mixture is distributed along a spray bar to each
cylinder in equal amounts. Throttle body injection was
used by manufacturers, particularly domestics, as a transi-
tion between the traditional carburetor and the more
powerful, and more efficient, multi-port injection.

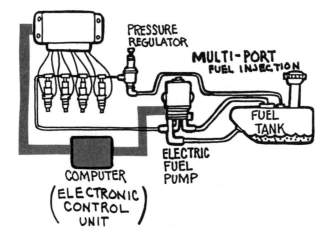

In multi-port fuel injection, a separate injector, which
looks like a fat spark plug (that's where the resemblance
ends) and acts like an atomizer, mixes and delivers an
individualized ideal diet of air and fuel for each cylinder.
The microscopic hole through which the air and fuel mixture is delivered is so tiny it has to made with a laser
beam!

A whiz-bang on-board computer, an electronic brain, is
responsible for the success of fuel injection at accomplish-
ing difficult, even contradictory, tasks. A microprocessor
called an electronic control unit or system receives information from tiny feelers (sensors) located throughout the
car. The sensors feed back information about many things,
including the speed of the engine, the temperature of the
air, and the density of the air and gasoline. With this
input, the computer then determines the optimal ratio of
air and fuel. Here's an example of how it works. One particularly important sensor, the oxygen sensor, monitors
the richness or leaness of the fuel mixture. If it finds that
the mixture has too much fuel (is too rich) or has too little
fuel (is too lean), it tells the computer this in the form of
lightning fast Morse code, which is translated into a number. The computer reads the number and goes to its data
base where alternative air/fuel combinations ideally
suited for different driving conditions are stored. Just as
with all computers, information is stored in memory boxes
called cells which are set up in a gridlike pattern, similar
to the map of a city. The streets are the pathways along
which the electronic impulses travel. The computer selects
the best air/fuel mixture for the specific driving condition
at that moment and sends electronic impulses to the injectors, changing the length of time that they remain open or
turning them on more frequently, thus changing the
amount of fuel delivered, and fine-tuning the mixture as
many as ten times in a second!

MICRO PROCESSOR
OR
COMPUTER

DATA

   There are, however, limits to this self-adjusting system.
Trouble occurs when the numbers exceed a certain range.
The computer only stores a specific number of air/fuel

alternatives. Consequently, when the sensors feed back information that exceeds their capacity to respond, the driver usually notices engine performance problems. It is then time for a professional to step in and check out the system with an engine analyzer.

Computer Troubleshooting

By connecting an engine analyzer to the on-board computer, the technician is able to run a general systems test or enter specific symptoms and have the analyzer respond with diagnostic messages suggesting the most likely causes. A single analyzer may have hundreds of messages, which take the form of numbered codes that are flashed on a screen. The technician then may make a precise adjustment or replace a faulty sensor or other computer component. Hopefully, when the check is run again, the code displayed will indicate that the problem has been corrected. If not, the test will have to be run again and the next likely set of causes reviewed. Beginning with the basics—dirty or sticking injectors, clogged filters, and leaks in the many hoses that help the system to operate correctly—the professional mechanic should be able to track down the culprit(s) and correct the problem.

But what happens when the symptom will not duplicate itself for the benefit of the mechanic? Just as our aching teeth seem to get better whenever we come within 100 yards of a dentist, often a car seems to get better the closer we get to the repair shop. Unfortunately, there are no panaceas for this annoying problem. Naturally, if it is an intermittent problem, you will want the technician to road test the car in order to re-create it, but even that may not help if the car isn't willing to cooperate. If the symptom appears again after the car has been returned to you with a bogus clean bill of health, gather as much information as possible about the problem and write it down so that you remember to tell the technician everything. Even details that seem remote may be important.

You will need to become a detective with a sharp eye, ear, nose, and memory. Is it a sound—a click, a clunk, a slap, a tick? Is it an odor? Does it smell like bad eggs, gasoline, or burning rubber? Is the engine changing its routine?

Is it hesitating (not responding for a split second when you step on the gas pedal)? Is the engine missing, is the regular beating of its heart skipping? Is the problem only happening on cold days, hots days, days when there is thunder and lightning? Does it happen only in third gear, or only as you shift gears? Does it happen only after you have driven five miles at highway speeds, or before you've driven five miles? Every single solitary detail that may appear to be insignificant may have a bearing on revealing the problem's cause. For more on communicating symptoms, see chapter 12.

Remember that all computer engine analyzers are not equal. Different shops have very different levels of sensitivity in their diagnostic equipment. Some will respond with such a long list of possible causes that it would take forever to narrow the real culprit down by trial and error. Furthermore, the same equipment can be operated differently. One technician may use the equipment to test one system only, perhaps missing a problem in another system that isn't the likely source but is a possible one. Just as you would with a medical doctor, if the cause of your problem is not diagnosed within a reasonable time, a second opinion is always a good idea.

Obviously, fuel injection won't yield its secrets to the ordinary person equipped with a rusty screwdriver who happens along to help you if you're broken down by the side of the road. It's much more likely that person will open the hood, close the hood, and ask you where you would like to have the car towed for repairs. Preventive maintenance with this system is essential. Carburetors and fuel injection systems are checked out and adjusted according to the service schedule in your owner's manual. Ignoring or postponing scheduled service is asking for trouble.

If you're wondering whether your car is fuel injected or carbureted, check your owner's manual, ask your mechanic, or look to see if there is a decal on the car with the letters FI or EFI.

Important Facts about Fuel

If the carburetor or fuel injection system is adjusted properly, if the air and fuel filters are changed at their recommended intervals, and if the fuel pump system is in working order, are the first two parts of the "diet" now complete? Not quite. First, take a look at the illustration of the fuel tank (p. 18). See those little dots at the bottom of the gas tank? Now, hold that thought for a moment while I tell you a story.

As a teenager, five brothers and I used the family car, so it was a common scene to hear Dad yell as he slammed the front door, "Who used the damn car last? And why didn't you put gas in it?" Mercifully, by the time he recited the litany of all our names, he had often forgotten the infraction. There's no telling how many times he was stranded by our selective reading of the gas gauge. After I graduated from school, I began driving my first car. It was a little black Volkswagen that I dearly loved and still fondly remember. And it taught me a lot about gasoline.

Despite the fact that my little car got about 172 miles to the gallon, I habitually refused to put in more than 47 cents worth of gas at any one time. This had a lot to do with the fact that I never seemed to have more than 47 cents to spend at one time. Furthermore, using the skills I had learned as a teenager, I meticulously estimated exactly how much gas was in the tank at any given time. Using these calculations, I frequently arrived at a gas station with little more than fumes in the tank. The car would struggle, sputter, cough, and die in front of the pump, and I would emerge triumphantly, congratulating myself for doing another swell job of squeezing every last drop out of the tank. I then pumped in another 47 cents worth and off I'd go for another two weeks. It was not until several years later that I discovered what my calculations had really wrought.

Now, remember those tiny dots in the illustration of the fuel tank? Those harmless-looking specks are actually flotsam and jetsam, pieces of dirt and metal filings that gradually accumulate at the bottom of any gas tank. There the particles rest, harmless, until the fuel level in the tank gets so low that the fuel pump sucks them out along with the last few drops of gasoline. Like the food particles that are left in the kitchen sink after the dishes have been washed, all the residual particles want to go down the drain with the last bit of water.

To continue the story, every time I arrived at the station with the gauge on EMPTY, the dirt and other contaminants at the bottom of the tank had been forced along the fuel lines to the fuel filter, which quickly clogged and needed replacement. I bought a lot of unnecessary fuel filters. On one occasion, the filter was so clogged that no gas was able to pass through to the carburetor. The car sputtered and died, and I got to pay for a tow, a new filter, and a carburetor cleanout!

Even after I discovered the expensive consequences of my 47-cent habit, I couldn't seem to quit. Desperate, I began to pretend that if the tank showed ¼ full, it was actually empty. I am happy to say I am finally cured. Now I habitually practice the second nicest thing anyone can do for a car: keep the tank as full as possible (I'll tell you the first in chap. 6). Remember, gas is not good to the last drop.

Gas Line Freeze-up
There's another good reason for keeping the tank full which is especially important in areas where temperatures drop dramatically at night. The same condensation process that produces dew on the grass on an autumn morning causes water droplets to form inside the gas tank. Most tanks are sealed with a special rust-inhibiting coating so that the water does not cause rust. No problem then, you might say? Well, it isn't, until the first bitter cold morning of the winter season, after you've driven the car 15 to 20 minutes and the car coughs, sputters, and dies. What may have happened is that those water droplets turned to ice crystals, moved along the gas line with the gas, and clogged

GRASS

FUEL TANK

the tiny openings of the carburetor or fuel injector nozzles.

The solution for gas line freeze-up? Wait until spring when it thaws? It's unlikely that will work unless you have a very flexible schedule. You can avoid the problem altogether by keeping the tank as full as possible, especially at night when the condensation process will be accelerated. The more space in the tank, the more space for condensation to form.

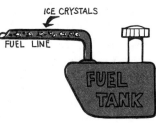

ICE CRYSTALS

FUEL LINE

FUEL TANK

But if it's too late for prevention, and you think water droplets may have already formed in the tank, a can of dry gas is an inexpensive way to prevent gas line freeze-up, providing that the water is in a quantity small enough not to unbalance the diet so much that the car wouldn't have started in the first place. The way dry gas works is clever. It's obvious from the pictures of an oil spill that oil and water don't mix. Gasoline is oil based and so it doesn't combine with water (the water remains at the bottom of the tank); however, oil and alcohol do mix, and dry gas is alcohol. Alcohol and water also mix, so when added to water-contaminated gas, the dry gas (alcohol) causes the gas and water to mix together in the tank. The water and gas mixture then moves through the gas line toward the heat of the engine, where the water eventually evaporates.

GAS H2O — MIX NO

ALCOHOL H2O — MIX YES

ALCOHOL GAS — MIX YES

ALCOHOL GAS H2O — MIX YES

The most important thing to know about dry gas is that it's a remedy for a problem. It's similar to taking a pain reliever: you wouldn't take one every day unless you were treating a specific symptom. Additives of any kind in sufficient quantities may upset the delicate balance of the gas mixture, so be judicious. Ask your mechanic what type he or she recommends if you feel there is a problem, and read the directions carefully.

Contaminated Fuel

Gasoline comes in many varieties and qualities. It is a widely held belief among the mechanics who care for today's cars that dirty gasoline is responsible for a number of "driveability" problems. This vague term includes rough running, poor acceleration, hesitation, and a vast array of other engine performance problems that cannot be readily diagnosed or easily fixed.

In recent years, the microscopic openings of fuel injector nozzles and their sensitive sensors have increased the need for squeaky clean gasoline free of contaminants. Many petroleum manufacturers have addressed this problem by adding detergents to their products. The best advice I have to avoid performance problems that may be fuel related is to buy gas with detergent. (This will be indicated on the pump or in the advertising.) Find a reputable retailer who does a fairly high volume of business (not one that looks as though the Adams Family runs it, complete with cobwebs on the pump handles from lack of use), and buy from the same station whenever possible. In this way, you can isolate at least one variable that affects performance. If you have a minor engine performance problem, try switching brands of gasoline (even if you do get a kick out of seeing who buys the pickled eggs at your station). And notice whether there's a change for the better or worse in the way the car drives. Watch out for water in the tank which may have come from a contaminated fuel supply. If your fuel filter is filled with water, and you're only buying from one station, you will at least know where not to buy!

Vapor Lock

The additives in today's gasolines have raised their volatility (the ability to change from a liquid to a vapor). During hot weather, gasoline may actually boil, thus turning to a vapor that fuel pumps can't move. The result is vapor lock, an engine that is starved for fuel, the symptoms of which are rough running, loss of power, and in some instances, stalling. Electric in-tank fuel pumps located far from the heat of the engine provide more constant pressure to the system and have alleviated the problem in most cars, but if yours isn't one of those and vapor lock is a problem, try switching from your regular brand of gasoline to another reputable brand. If that doesn't work, it's possible that the fuel lines can be rerouted so they are farther removed from the hot spots of the engine.

What about Regular Unleaded and Super Unleaded?

In the mid-1970s, the EPA, in response to its research findings that the lead in gasoline was harmful to our health, began mandating the use of emission control components. One component, the catalytic converter, was actually fouled by lead. The problem was that tetra-ethyl lead was gasoline's chief octane enhancer.

The octane rating of a gasoline (you'll see it displayed on the front of each pump) refers to its resistance to knocking. Ideally, when gasoline burns, it should do so evenly throughout the entire combustion chamber. If the gasoline has too low an octane number, it may burn unevenly or explode at the wrong time. The smooth up-and-down motion of the rapidly firing pistons will be exposed to a vibration or shock. The engine will still run, but the sound

SPARK KNOCK   NORMAL COMBUSTION

you may hear is a metallic rattling, pinging, clicking, or knocking, like marbles or ball bearings hitting together. The higher the octane, the slower and smoother the gasoline will burn and the less likely it is to burn irregularly and cause knocking or pinging.

Gasoline manufacturers had to come up with a substitute for lead, a gram of which per gallon raises the octane rating six numbers. They developed tertiary butyl alcohol and other octane enhancers to create unleaded gasoline. Unfortunately, not all unleaded gasolines meet the octane requirements of many newer cars. Premium unleaded gasolines generally do.

Should you buy super unleaded gasoline? Maybe yes, maybe no. So how do you know for sure if you should be paying the extra cents per gallon for premium unleaded? First, if your dealer or owner's manual recommends premium unleaded, or a gas with an equivalent octane rating, use it. The dealers' and manufacturers' advice is based on their extensive experience with the engine performance of your particular car. In other words, like it or not, your car's engine may simply require the more expensive premium unleaded gas for engine performance that is knock or ping-free. If you haven't received any caveats from your mechanic, or manual, then consider the following experiment.

Fill up with a tank of regular unleaded gasoline. Test drive the car without the radio, your kids, or noisy pets.

Listen for any new engine sound. If you hear pinging or knocking, make a note to switch to super or premium unleaded next time you buy gas. If the rattle or pinging goes away, stick with the super unleaded.

If you've received no warning from dealer, mechanic, or owner's manual, there's no knocking or pinging, and you really have listened, then you should be able to safely use regular unleaded. Under most circumstances, you shouldn't have to use a more expensive gasoline because your car probably doesn't really need it.

If you're already using premium unleaded and still hear pinging or knocking, it's a good idea to have the car checked out by a mechanic. Some pinging is normal in newer cars and is considered an acceptable trade-off for the fuel-efficient mixture your engine may be burning; however, excessive pinging or rattling can cause engine damage and may be the result of a different problem, detonation. Unfortunately, there are about a billion different causes of detonation. If there is any question in your mind whether your car has a harmless or harmful ping, rattle, or knock, ask your dealer or mechanic to decide by taking it for a test drive.

What about the occasional use of a tank of super unleaded? It can't hurt, and it might help. Even though your engine may not need the premium unleaded with its higher octane rating, it may appreciate the special additives, especially the detergents, that the premium gas has to offer.

That covers the first two parts of the diet. If the carburetor or fuel injection system is running properly, all the filters are in working order, and the gasoline you're using is the correct octane for your car and is free of contaminants, your car is headed in the right direction for smooth running.

3

Ignition and Charging:
The Diet, Part 3

"Ignition," once I had learned its meaning, was another automotive term that convinced me that cars were not mystical. Ignition comes from the word *ignite*, to set on fire, and what better device for setting something on fire than a spark? The job of your car's ignition system, therefore, is to add a spark to the explosive air and fuel mixture that the carburetor or fuel injection system has taken such pains to create. This, as promised, is the third and final part of the engine's diet.

The journey of the ignition's spark is circuitous. It begins at the battery and ends at the spark plug in the combustion chamber. If anything happens to interrupt its journey along the route, the car will not start at all, will start with difficulty, or if it starts, will run unevenly.

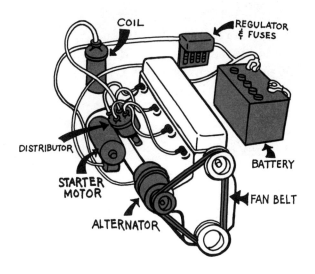

When you turn the ignition key on, it sends a wake-up call to a small but wiry electrical current that has been snoozing in the battery. The battery, which supplies electrical energy to start the engine running and provides power to the accessories even when it is not, is like a clothes closet for electricity. Instead of suits, shirts, and shoes, however, this closet stores a little more than 12 volts of electrical current. Those 12 volts aren't much in electrical terms (your home generally uses 110 and 220 volts), but before their journey is over, they will have been magnified many

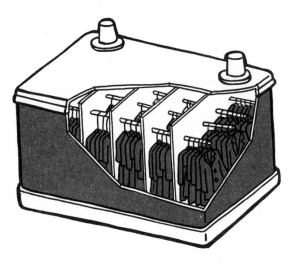

thousands of times. You might say they have an explosive future ahead of them.

From the battery, the 12 volts travel within a rubber-covered wire to the ignition switch and then to the coil, where they get a big boost. The coil turns those puny 12 volts into super spark—30,000 to 60,000 volts of hot electricity. That's enough voltage to curl your hair without a curling iron.

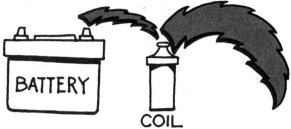

BATTERY

COIL

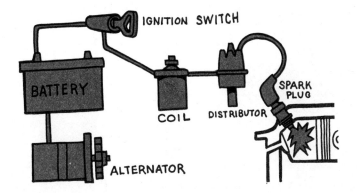

IGNITION SWITCH

BATTERY

COIL

DISTRIBUTOR

SPARK PLUG

ALTERNATOR

From the coil, the super spark moves to the distributor, which acts like a card dealer. The distributor deals an equal portion of the fortified super spark to each cylinder (the hollow tubes that are cut into the engine block and house the pistons). There, a spark plug, located at the top of each cylinder, receives the spark. This is one card dealer whose honesty you need not question. He never deals off the bottom of the deck.

Super spark now jumps, or arcs, across the opening or gap at the tip of the spark plug. This is how the sparking plug got its name. The second that spark jumps the gap and reaches the air and fuel mixture in the cylinder. . . Kaboom! It's like dropping a match into a container of gasoline. And the whole ignition trip takes place in a fraction of a second.

If this ignition business is beginning to sound like a little more excitement than you had in mind, remember that once the spark has jumped, all of the following action takes place inside the engine block. This heavy metal case, made of cast iron or aluminum, is surrounded and sealed by tough insulating materials called gaskets that keep most of the noise and compression forces inside.

If the car is tuned correctly, the sound you will hear as you turn the ignition key to ON and the first spark is successfully delivered is "vrrooon-vrrooon." The engine should now be running smoothly. If the car is not tuned correctly and if all the systems and their component parts are not in top working order, you may be hearing a lot of "rrreh-rrrehs" before you finally get a "vrrooon-vrrooon." If things are really fouled up, you may never hear any

SPARKPLUG

GAP

sound at all. Here are some important facts about the ignition system that can help make yours more reliable and trouble-free. Let's begin where it all begins, at the heart of the ignition system, the battery.

How to Avoid Cold Weather "No-starts"

The scene is your home. It's 8:30 a.m. The temperature outside is a crisp 12 degrees F. This is the most important day of your life. Your 9:00 a.m. business appointment represents a year's worth of hard work; all you have to do is show up to sign the papers and the client is yours. But everything (and I do mean everything) that can go wrong, goes wrong. The blackberry jam slurps down your only clean silk blouse. You catch your finger in the toaster, step in the cat's water. The milk you put in your coffee slowly

floats to the top and curdles. You come screaming out of the house at about Mach 6, hurl yourself into the front seat of the car, turn the key, and—nothing. It's so quiet you could hear a worm burp. You slowly raise your eyes to heaven and say (among other things), "Why me?" "Why today?"

The answer will come not from the sky above but from beneath the hood. Your battery may have chosen this very moment to demonstrate that it doesn't like cold weather. Despite its willingness to start day after day, year after year, this first cold day of the fall season may have tested its starting ability once and for all.

Now you may never get to savor the fruits of your work. And it all might have been avoided. If you had scheduled an appointment to have your ignition system checked out (not tuned up) by a professional mechanic before the cold weather set in, you probably would have heard that your battery was in the twilight of its years. You probably would have heard that the chemicals needed for the storage of sufficient voltage to start the car were running low. You probably would have heard that the next set of cold temperatures might send that geriatric battery to its well-deserved electrical grave.

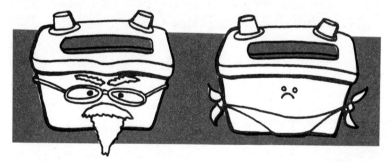

That would have been the time to begin shopping for a new battery—from a mechanic you trust, one who services your car on a regular basis, or, if you're a Do-It-Yourselfer, from a reputable retailer. Your friendly tow truck driver may have only one brand of battery—the Zillion Dollar brand—and you're in no position to quibble.

The Battery

The ability of the battery to successfully provide the electrical energy necessary to start the car depends on a lot of things, including the size and age of the battery and the outside air temperature. Like many of us, batteries don't work as well in cold weather. When the outside temperature is 80 degrees F, a battery is 100 percent efficient. On a nice day, whatever chemicals are left inside will be maximally efficient; however, that same battery at 0 degrees F is only 40 percent efficient. In other words, over 60 percent of its ability to store the electricity needed to start the car is temporarily absent!

For a healthy battery, with lots of chemicals left in it, there's no problem. Forty percent of a lot is a lot. A healthy battery has plenty of energy to spare. For an older battery that has started a car many times and has used up a lot of its chemicals, however, losing 60 percent of its starting ability—when it didn't have too much to begin with—may put that battery right over the edge.

A battery is constructed of a hard rubberized or plastic casing. Inside there are usually six rooms, or cells; each cell stores a little over 2 volts of electricity within two metal plates made of different lead compounds. Remember from science class that all objects have either a negative or positive charge and that unlike charges attract and like charges repel? One of the plates in each cell has a positive charge. The other plate has a negative charge. The plates

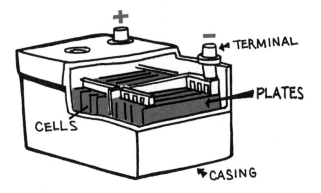

sit in a liquid solution of water and sulfuric acid called electrolyte, which, when activated by the ignition key's wake-up call, causes the opposite charges of the different plate metals to react chemically.

The chemical reaction that results from the attraction

of the opposite charges causes the small particles that make up the elements and compounds within the battery to move. It is this particle movement that is the chemical energy to be converted into electrical energy. As the battery generates electrical energy, it ages with use. The sulfuric acid in the electrolyte solution is absorbed into the metal plates, where it forms a hard crusty deposit, leaving a weakened electrolyte that is mostly water. Once they reach a certain thickness, the deposits, which appear as a white powdery substance on the battery's posts or terminals that protrude from its top or side, block the passage of the electrical current through the battery.

When the plates become completely covered, the battery discharges and can no longer provide the necessary electrical energy to start the car. If the battery is not too far gone, an electrical current is run through it in the opposite direction (a charging direction) by a battery charger, and the lead sulfate disappears from the plates and returns to the water, raising the amount of sulfuric acid in the electrolyte. The battery may get a new life.

BATTERY CHARGER

Conventional and Maintenance-free Batteries
Before a battery can be fairly tested to determine if it needs replacement, it must be given a charge. If you accidentally leave the lights or radio on in your car overnight and discover a dead battery, it doesn't necessarily mean you need a new one. The battery may be temporarily discharged and may only need to be recharged.

To determine the state of charge for a battery, a hydrometer is used. This device, which resembles a turkey baster, measures the amount of sulfuric acid remaining in the solution. The resulting measurement is referred to as the battery's specific gravity reading. The test is like taking the battery's pulse. An acceptable specific gravity reading for a fully charged battery would be above 1.225 depending on the temperature. If the reading is lower than that and it is otherwise healthy, the battery should be fully charged before further testing takes place.

Once it is determined that the battery is fully charged, a load tester completes the examination. It's called a load tester because it simulates the "load" or electrical need to which the battery must respond. In this case, that need is

the amount of energy, measured in voltage, it takes for the
starter motor to start your car's engine at 0 degrees for 15
seconds. In other words, it pretends that it's your starter
motor trying to start the car on a cold day—the battery's
toughest job. A fully charged battery that cannot produce
this minimum voltage should be replaced.

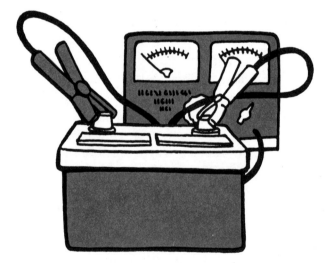

With conventional "low maintenance" batteries you
should also check (or pay for full-service and have someone
else check) the level of the electrolyte by removing the
plastic protective covers. The solution inside should reach
the bottom of the plastic filler necks and pucker a little,

The ignition wires, as well as other ignition components (listed in your owner's manual), should be replaced once every three or four years, or whenever your owner's manual recommends.

The spark plugs may be eroded to the point where the spark doesn't jump, the air/fuel mixture doesn't ignite, and the engine never starts or runs roughly. A spark plug's tip may be covered with carbon or oil deposits, or its gap may be too wide or too narrow. Any of these conditions will interrupt the spark's journey. If the plugs are merely dirty or incorrectly gapped, they can be cleaned or adjusted. On many newer cars, spark plugs are designed to go 50,000 miles or more before replacement is necessary. On older cars, however, the plugs are generally replaced at more frequent regular intervals regardless of their visible condition. Check your owner's manual for recommended interval changes.

Computerized Ignitions

Today, most cars have computerized ignitions. The same computer (electronic control unit) that provides a better

COMPUTERIZED IGNITION

air/fuel mixture has also taken over coordinating the functions of the traditional ignition system. Many of the traditional ignition components, including the "points," metal arms that open and close, the condenser, a tiny sponge that absorbs excess current, and on some ignition systems, the

distributor, have been replaced. Sensors feed back information to the computer's brain so that it can determine when the spark should arrive and how hot it should be when it gets there.

The spark gets to its destination faster, hotter, and with greater accuracy than it did with traditional ignitions. This more efficient electronic ignition with its extremely hot spark is one reason newer cars often run, but not with impunity, even when they are in desperate need of service. Ignition components that are not working properly cause fuel mileage to drop and the starter and battery to work harder and wear prematurely. Like the fuel injection system, sophisticated diagnostic equipment is necessary to test the computerized ignition components.

The Charging System

Earlier, I mentioned that the battery doesn't make electricity, it only stores it. Once the spark has done its work, that is, exploded the first air/fuel mixture to move the pistons, and the engine is running, it is the job of the alternator (the modern-day version of a generator), which is a motor that makes electricity, to take over as the power source and replace the electricity used up by the heavy demands of the start.

An alternator works on the same principle as a checking account. If you only withdraw and never deposit money, eventually the account will show a big goose egg. Since the battery uses up its stored supply of electrical energy to start the car, it needs a deposit to cover the withdrawal. The alternator deposits electricity into the battery's account while the car is running so that the battery is always ready to start your car. It also provides power for everything else in your electrically hungry car while the engine is running, including the radio, windshield wipers, and lights.

A voltage regulator is another important part of this savings and withdrawal system. It reduces current to the alternator once the engine picks up speed. This keeps the alternator from overcharging the battery. If the alternator works overtime, the battery will be overcharged, resulting in a loss of water and an early demise. If the alternator works too little, the battery will eventually discharge and will be too drained to start the car.

As is true of many of the components in your car, the alternator is activated by a rubber belt that runs on a pulley, similar to a clothesline pulley. The belt is attached to the turning crankshaft of the engine. Assuming the alternator and belt are in working order, whenever the engine is running, the belt turns and the alternator makes electricity to recharge the battery and to power the accessories.

Belts

The average car today has from three to five belts, but some newer cars have only one. They all contribute to keeping your car out of the breakdown lane. As belts wear from the constant rotational movement of the pulley, they stretch and get thinner. As the thinner belt sinks deeper into the pulley, you may hear a high squeaking sound (similar to a tennis shoe on a gym floor) or a squeal (an extended version of a squeak) coming from under the hood. If you do hear such a sound, be sure to have it checked out by your mechanic.

Problems also arise when a belt has the wrong tension. Incorrect tension causes the belt to wear faster, because its slipping action generates more friction and heat. A slipping belt may also cause the component it drives to wear faster, or to malfunction. The wrong tension may also cause glazing, a hard icelike substance that forms on the inside of the belt and never melts. Glazing causes the belt to slip and reduces its ability to keep it in contact with the pulley and do its job.

Belts that appear brittle, flaky, or cracked should be replaced. Regardless of their outward appearance, they should all be replaced every three to four years or whenever your owner's manual says.

When the belts are replaced, be sure to ask your mechanic to return the old ones to you. Label each one; they all look alike after a short time. Put them in a plastic bag and throw them in the back of the car as insurance against belt failure on the road. Belts come in all different sizes and shapes, depending on the make and model of your car. If you're stuck in East Cupcake on a Friday night with a broken belt, the likelihood that the local garage will have the particular belt you need is, as the mathematicians say, seriously small. How nice to reach into your emergency bag of tricks and pull out the correct belt instead of having to wait in a dingy motel with no cable television until a parts store or dealership opens on Monday. You can continue on your way; stop as soon as you can for a proper replacement, though.

What to Do If the Alternator Light Goes On

You're driving along the highway. It's night and your car's headlights go dim, dimmer, dimmest. The dashboard alternator light or battery symbol flashes, or the needle on the voltage gauge begins to read "Discharge." You try to remember. Is that the light I stop for? No. Yes. No. Can't remember.

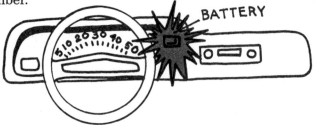

An alternator light that goes on or a gauge that indicates a discharge condition means more electricity is being used up than is being replaced. Eventually there's nothing left. The good news is it's probably not fatal, just massively inconvenient, especially if the car will not run at all. The rule is to get thee to a service station as soon as possible and reduce the use of as many accessories as you safely can. Obviously, if it's raining, you can't turn the windshield wipers off, but you can switch off the radio and maybe the heat. Any component that uses electricity is draining critical power from the noncharging battery. The hardest thing the electrical system has to do is start the car, so you don't want to turn the engine off unless it's absolutely necessary. Red alert! At this point you must pay careful attention to the other dashboard lights.

If another dash light comes on while you're trying to

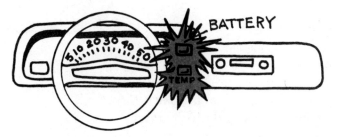

hobble to the nearest gas station, and it's a light or gauge that relates to engine temperature, you will need to stop the car as soon as you can get it safely off the road. The belt that drives the alternator often drives other important items like the water pump. If the water pump stops working (turn to chap. 5 for the reasons this might happen), it won't be long before the engine overheats, causing major damage and expensive repairs. If that second light is Engine Temperature, Temperature, or Coolant Sensor or is a gauge that shows the temperature moving into the danger zone, the engine is in danger of frying.

Important Information about Winter Driving

During the winter months we use more accessories—more heat, maybe even more radio—and typically take shorter trips. Add this to the battery's natural resistance to accept a charge in cold weather, and the charging system may never get a chance to build back up to full strength. Little by little, it discharges and may be drained completely without warning. This can happen despite all the charging components being in good working order. One of the kindest things you can do for your car, and one of the smartest things you can do for yourself, is to take your car for a 25- to 30-minute highway cruise—not stop-and-go traffic. Doing this once a week revitalizes the charging sysysm and burns off many of the unwanted deposits that are the natural by-products of the combustion process. It's like giving your car a good aerobic workout or taking it for a brisk walk. Along with a well-balanced diet it will go a long way toward keeping it in shape and preventing automotive heart attacks.

A Tune-up

No automotive term is more abused, overused, and misunderstood. And it's no wonder with the changes that have taken place in cars over the last 20 years. What any backyard mechanic with a few simple tools could do 15 years ago is today the domain of schooled technicians armed with computerized machines and huge manuals.

It used to be that a tune-up meant a twice a year change of the spark plugs, points, and filters, and adjustment of the carburetor and timing. (We'll talk more about timing in chap. 4.) Now we have to deal with fuel injection, computerized ignition (whose spark plugs last five times longer than they once did), and emission controls, all of which require periodic inspection to ensure they are operating properly.

You won't find this information under the heading "Tune-up" in your owner's manual. What you will find there is a long list of things all good car owners ought to do every so many weeks, months, years, or miles—otherwise known as "scheduled service." Hidden somewhere in all that information are the components of what used to be, and still sometimes is, referred to as a tune-up. If it's supposed to be done every 7,000 to 30,000 miles and it directly concerns the performance of your car's engine (air, fuel, spark), it's probably part of a tune-up.

While the term "tune-up" may be an anachronism, you will probably continue to see it used to describe the routine replacement of spark plugs, filters, and other air, fuel, and ignition-related parts, plus a precise series of tests and adjustments to regain maximum engine performance. A tune-up may also involve battery service, timing, idle speed, vacuum and compression checks, pollution control systems, and belts and hoses. A tune-up does not include an oil change (or even check!), lubrication, brakes, transmission, steering and suspension components, tire rotation, wiper blade replacement, or tightening the screws on your license plate. While you may find it very convenient to get these maintenance chores done at the same time you have the car in for a tune-up, you will probably need to specifically request them.

By keeping your car on the recommended schedule for service listed in your owner's manual, you can stop worrying about tuneups. The result should be a quick-starting, smooth-running engine that gets the best mileage it can. A well-maintained engine can save as many as 35 gallons of gasoline each year, thus making some contribution toward paying for itself.

Better engine performance and gas mileage are but two good reasons to stay with scheduled service. Another good reason is that it may be a requirement of your warranty. To keep from voiding your warranty, you should follow, to the letter, the car maker's recommendations for regular maintenance and service. If the routine maintenance is not done as recommended, you could wind up paying for a major engine repair out of your own pocket. That assumes that the manufacturer's representative can demonstrate that the problem is causally related to the neglected maintenance procedure. Even if your car is not under warranty, it is still a good idea to follow your owner's manual specifications. What you'll find there could add years to your car's life, keep your bank balance healthy, and cure your insomnia.

Need more reasons? How about a cold dark night on a lonely road and a stalled engine? Or an important appointment and a car that won't start. And then there are those "read 'em and weep" repair bills, or tow charges for the rich and famous.

Stalling, hard starting, running rough at idle, hesitation, surging, misfiring, sluggishness, and a dramatic change in the gas mileage are all pleas from your car for maintenance. (See chap. 12 for more about keeping track of your gas mileage.) Ignore them and eventually your car will force you to get one. It will break down.

The cost of scheduled service will vary depending on a variety of things. What tests, adjustments, and repairs were done, the make, model, and year of your car, and even the area of the country in which you live determine the price. Call a couple of places if you want to be sure that the price you are quoted for service is in the fair ball park. And be sure you know exactly what is included in the price you are quoted. If your service is done correctly, your engine should run smoothly, your gas mileage should be back to normal, and any annoying engine-related performance problems should go away.

Performance Problems

Let's pretend, however, that you've been keeping your car on its maintenance schedule and you're experiencing performance problems; your car is coughing, sputtering, speeding up or slowing down when you haven't changed the pressure on the accelerator (surging), hesitating when you accelerate, running rough, hard starting, or stalling.

Do not assume that scheduled maintenance will automatically fix the problem. If you went to your doctor for your yearly checkup and you have been having severe headaches for over a month, would you expect that the doctor would discover the problem without your communicating the symptoms? No, you wouldn't expect the doctor to be a mind reader. You'd carefully describe where the pain was, how often it occurred, and what specific circumstances you could relate that might throw some light on the problem.

In the same way, when you bring your car in for scheduled service and there is a performance problem, be sure to tell the mechanic or service writer about it. Supply as many pertinent details as you can. Doing this faithfully will go a long way toward keeping you out of the shop until the next scheduled service. (See chap. 13 for more information about dealing with your mechanic or service writer.)

We have now looked at the diet in its entirety. The engine's plate contains a well-balanced meal. Air, fuel, and a hot spark are being mixed together in the correct proportions, resulting in the explosions that will cause the pistons to move up and down and the tires to eventually go round and round. In chapter 4, we'll look at how the engine metabolizes this diet and why it is so important that the spark be delivered at just the right time.

4

Timing, Compression, Exhaust, and Emissions

Timing and Compression

Timing. Fred Astaire and Ginger Rogers had it. All successful dancers have it. So do engines that run well. Timing is coordination. It is more than one person or part acting in unison to create a desired result. For dancers, the desired result is simple enough—present the audience with a graceful and tight series of movements. For cars, the desired result is to make the engine run smoothly, powerfully, and efficiently.

To accomplish this model of performance, correct timing or coordination must take place among the hundreds of engine components that create, combine, compress, and explode the engine's air/fuel/spark diet. Each component

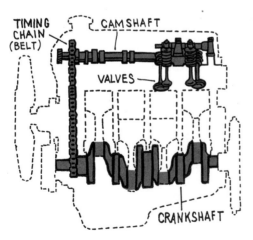

acts like a dancer in a chorus line. Each must know the part perfectly; if one dancer is a second late in the execution of a step, the entire performance will suffer, the director will not be happy, and the audience will not be pleased. In a chorus line, everyone must work together for a smooth effect. The same is true for the engine of your car. All the components must work together if the performance is to be smooth and error-free. The fact that your engine performs smoothly with the regularity it does is perhaps more surprising than the fact that occasionally it doesn't.

To understand timing—and the object of its affection, compression—we need to meet a few more of the working components of the engine. Keep in mind that we will discuss only those with speaking parts. There are many more in the chorus line which do not get marquee billing. Without them, however, the performance wouldn't be possible.

To "start" things off, there is the appropriately named starter motor. As you turn the ignition key to the ON position to start the car, a message is transmitted to the battery to send its electrical current over hill and dale to the spark plug. At the same time, the ignition key sends another signal to the starter, a small but powerful electrical motor that performs heroically until the engine fires.

Heroically, you ask? Judge for yourself. The starter's one distinctive feature is its head—a small, round, metal, toothed wheel or gear, specifically, a Bendex gear. Attached to this gear is an arm, or lever, called a solenoid. When the ignition key is turned to ON, this arm pushes the Bendex gear forward so that it meshes with a large heavy disc called the flywheel. The flywheel also has teeth in the form of its ring gear. The flywheel is attached to the crankshaft, the big bent bar that holds onto the pistons. When the flywheel turns, the crankshaft turns. When the crankshaft turns, the pistons move up and down.

With the ignition key on, the starter motor sticks its

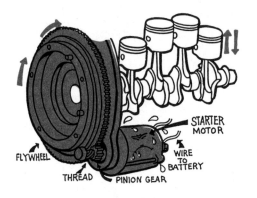

neck out and begins pushing that heavy flywheel around in circles. The crankshaft, because it is attached to the flywheel, begins to turn. The pistons, because they're attached to the crankshaft by metal arms called connecting rods, start to move up and down. If this is beginning to look more like the Keystone Kops than a chorus line, take heart. We still don't have all the actors on stage yet.

The Valve Train

Enter the valves. Look at the top of each cylinder, the hollow tubes that house the pistons. Located in the top part of the engine's metal casing, the head, you will see flanking the spark plug, like guards at the entrance to each cylinder, objects that look like upside-down golf tees—the valves. These valves are actually one-way doors, similar to those in your heart which allow blood to flow in one direction only. Each cylinder has a minimum of two (an intake valve and an exhaust valve) and as many as four (two intake and two exhaust).

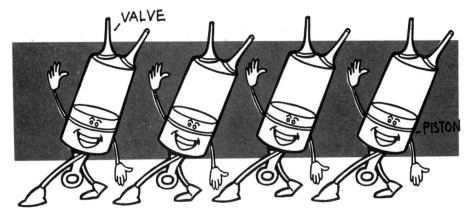

Valves regulate the flow of the fuel mixture into and out of the cylinders, but they never work solo. Depending on the specific design of the engine, hundreds of other bit parts, lumped under the heading "valve train," help the valves open and close. Among these bit part but essential players are springs, rocker arms, pushrods, and tappets. Smooth engine performance depends on the proper functioning of each.

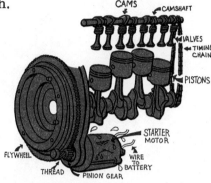

The valves are attached to the camshaft, a round metal bar that gets its name from its metal bumps, or lobes, called cams. The camshaft is attached to the crankshaft by a timing chain or belt. Because these two bars, crankshaft and camshaft, are attached to one another, when one turns the other does as well. Specifically, the camshaft turns at half the speed of the crankshaft. In other words, the crankshaft will rotate twice in the time it takes the camshaft to go around once.

As the camshaft turns, its lobes push against the valves, forcing them to slide up and down within metal shells (sleeves) called valve guides. Consequently, the valves open and close. Intake valves open to let the unburned fuel mixture into the upper area of the cylinders, the combustion chambers, the area within which the air/fuel mixture will be burned. The valves close tightly after the fuel mixture is allowed in and while it is burning. Exhaust valves open to permit the burned gases to exit after each burning, thus making room for a new air/fuel mixture to enter once again via the intake valve.

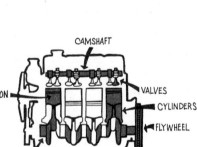

Meanwhile, back to the starter motor. The key is now in the ON position, and the starter is grunting and groaning, pushing the flywheel around. This action is timed to synchronize exactly with the emergence of the spark from the battery and its journey to the spark plug. As the starter motor turns the flywheel, the crankshaft attached to it turns, the pistons begin to move, and the intake valve opens. As the valve opens, the fuel and air mixture rushes into the combustion chamber, and the spark starts for home—the spark plug at the top of the combustion chamber. What you hear as you turn the key on—the "rrreh-rrreh" sound just before the first "vrooon-vrooon"—is the starter motor grunting and groaning. More about that later.

The Four-Stroke Cycle

Let's track the path of just one piston, #2, as it plays its part. Each of the other pistons will be doing the same thing but at a slightly different time. The key is now on, the starter is turning the flywheel, the crankshaft begins to turn. The piston, which is attached to the crankshaft, descends into the cylinder. On cue, the intake valve begins to open—*creeeeek*. The piston now acts like a big straw sucking the air/fuel mixture into the cylinder through the open valve—*whoosh*. The valve closes. The volatile mixture is now sealed inside the combustion chamber.

The starter motor is still pushing that big lump of a flywheel around, causing the crankshaft to turn and the piston to continue to descend. The piston eventually reaches the bottom of the cylinder, where its downward motion is reversed due to the continuing movement of the crankshaft. The piston now, with valves shut tight, begins the climb back up to the top of the cylinder. Now for the fun part.

As the piston moves higher into the cylinder, it begins to squeeze or compress the fuel mixture into a smaller and smaller space. The air/fuel mixture is beginning to feel like the heroine in an old horror movie. The walls of the room in which she's held prisoner begin to close in on her for the ultimate squeeze play, and it looks like she's going to get smooshed! But unlike the heroine, who usually gets saved, the mixture doesn't. It gets squeezed or compressed into a fraction of its former space. It is this compression that causes the air/fuel mixture to react so powerfully once ignited.

So just before the piston reaches the top of the path of its travel, when the air/fuel mixture thinks it can't stand one more second of this compression, the spark is delivered—*Kablam! Kapooey! Kapow!* The densely packed fuel vapor explodes at the maximum point of compression with the force of many sticks of dynamite. The heated gases expand violently and push the piston down and away. The piston would be driven right out the bottom of the engine were it not firmly attached to the turning crankshaft by means of its connecting rod. Good thing, too, or we'd be forever stopping to pick them up off the pavement, making progress slow and very expensive.

The piston now acts like a reusable bullet. Its powerful and violent up-and-down motion happens over and over

again—as many as 100 times a second—until the engine is turned off or stalls. Do you know how fast you have to move to do anything 100 times in a second? We're talking about a long blink. The valves may open and close 100,000 times in an hour! Within a fraction of a second, all the pistons are going up and down at the same amazing speed but at different times in order to reduce the vibration that would be felt if they were all to ignite at once. Remember back in chapter 1 where we likened the movement of the pistons to that of a bicyclist's legs? Those legs just went from a smooth, slow pedal motion to a blur!

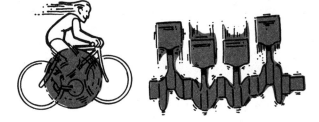

Each movement of a piston, up or down, is called a stroke. Although only one stroke actually produces power, it takes four strokes to make that happen. During Stroke 1, the intake stroke, the piston moves downward, drawing the fuel mixture in behind it. During Stroke 2, the compression stroke, the piston moves back up, compressing the fuel mixture, until the spark is delivered just before it reaches the top. During Stroke 3, the power stroke, the piston moves downward again as the gas ignites and expands. During Stroke 4, the exhaust stroke, which takes place after the gases are burned, the piston once again rises (this time because the piston next door has just fired, causing the crankshaft to turn again), and another valve, an exhaust valve, opens to expel the hot used gases. It takes these four movements of the piston to turn the crankshaft 2 revolutions and to produce the turning power of the engine, or "torque."

Ensuring Maximum Engine Performance

The camshaft and crankshaft must move like professional ballroom dancers coordinating the movement of the valves so that they open and close at exactly the right time. The intake valve should open so that a maximum amount of the unburned air/fuel mixture reaches the combustion chamber before compression takes place. The exhaust valve should then open so that a maximum of burned gases leave the chamber immediately after ignition takes place. If the valves open at any other time, the fuel mixture may be weak. If they open while combustion is taking place, a loss of power will result, and the exhaust valve may be burned by the excessive heat of the ignited gases or damaged by the piston movement, not to mention the danger to the catalytic converter, which won't appreciate those nasty hot gases spewing into it. If this happens, you may hear a loud backfire as the explosion escapes from the combustion chamber into the exhaust manifold.

The spark must be delivered to the spark plug at the correct moment—just before the piston reaches the top of the cylinder (TDC), having thoroughly compressed the air/fuel mixture. If the spark plug ignites the air/fuel mixture at any other time, for example, when the piston has already begun to descend, the piston will not be pushed as far. Consequently, the power that results will not be as great. All the players must fit *and* they must know their parts perfectly.

It is timing that coordinates this mass of movement among the engine's numerous parts, thus ensuring maximum compression, which results in maximum engine power, and fuel efficiency—two items that should be on every car owner's wish list. On most newer cars, the computer that mixes the air and fuel and makes certain that the spark is hot is responsible for timing. The computer receives information from the sensors about the delivery of the spark, the movement of the crankshaft, and the opening and closing of the valves, and adjusts accordingly. On cars without computers, timing is the result of coordination that takes place mechanically. With either system, timing is checked during regularly scheduled service.

The Starter

Now, for just a moment, let's return to that gutsy little starter. We left it turning the heavy flywheel around in circles. It's designed to carry an exceptionally heavy load for a few seconds. However, if there's a problem in one of the systems that creates and distributes the air/fuel/spark which causes the engine to start with difficulty, the starter has to work longer and harder than it should, causing it to overheat. Your regular scheduled service is usually the solution to a slow-starting engine. But be sure to describe any hard-starting problems to your mechanic or service writer. If your owner's manual doesn't call for service in the near future, make a special visit and have the problem corrected. Ask your starter to work longer hours by holding the ignition key on for more than 45 seconds, and you'll send it to an early grave while you foot the bill for its replacement.

At a time when electricity is pretty much taken for granted, electric starters hardly seem worthy of special notice, but without them, our automotive lives would look very different. Before modern starters were invented during the late 1800s, cars were started by manually turning a metal bar or crank that fit into a socket in the engine. It was often necessary to repeat this back-breaking task many times before the cranker successfully started the engine.

Especially in winter, when low temperatures thickened the engine oil into a gooey, jellylike substance that made all the internal parts move with great difficulty, 50 to 150 hand cranks were common before an engine would start. Consequently, people in cold climates often didn't drive their cars in the winter because of the great difficulty in starting them. Sometimes they even built a fire under the engine block to warm the engine oil so it would flow more easily. (This method proved to be very exciting: at times, the gasoline tank exploded.) Another common practice was to drain the engine oil into a container and then bring it into the house and set it next to the wood-stove, where it would be kept warm and remain thin enough to make starting easier. In the morning, it would be taken back out to the car and poured into the crankcase. What this method lacked in excitement it made up for in messiness.

Early engines were not only hard to start but they were also notorious for backfiring and causing the crank to jump back on the cranker, often breaking eyeglasses, jaws, noses, and anything else in its way. Besides being a tough job, starting cars was downright dangerous. The electric starter, while we may take it for granted, has definitely made life easier.

Heat and Wear

Combustion and its resulting heat—enough to heat a three-bedroom house at zero degrees—causes the pistons, cylinders, valves, block, and head to expand at different rates. If a piston were machined to the exact size of the cylinder, there wouldn't be enough clearance when it expanded for it to move at the breathtaking speeds it does. Space must be provided to allow for the expansion, but space would allow gases to escape from the combustion chamber and reduce compression and power. Therefore, pistons are surrounded by thin round metal hoops called rings. These rings expand into the combustion chamber, sealing it and scraping excess oil from the cylinder walls.

PISTON
RING

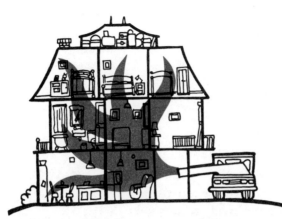

They permit movement but keep gases from escaping—acting like a seal as the engine heats up.

The rings experience tremendous wear as they move up and down with the pistons. Over time the metal wears thin, and the seal the ring forms is not as tight as it once was. Worn rings let gases escape and leave excess oil in the combustion chambers where it gets burned excessively and can sometimes be noticed coming from the tailpipe in the form of dark blue smoke.

Valves also wear over time, with serious consequences for compression. When they are new, valves close tightly, trapping the gases in the combustion chamber. But after opening and closing many hundreds of thousands of times, they wear. So they don't seal as tightly, gases escape, and the full force of combustion is diminished. Like a glass of carbonated soda that is left too long with the cap slightly ajar, the fizz just isn't the same. The result is a loss of power and an increase in oil consumption. You may notice the burning oil in the form of dark blue smoke coming from the tailpipe. The remedy may be to replace some of the worn internal parts with new ones.

It is not that your car's engine doesn't want heat. After all, a portion of that heat is the energy that is converted into power; another portion is used to burn off harmful deposits—the natural by-products of combustion. Some of the heat leaves the car as waste by way of the exhaust, but the remainder, which is excess heat, has to be regulated. It is the cooling system in combination with oil that keeps the engine's temperature correct. To understand how these temperature controls work—and why they sometimes don't—turn to chapters 5 and 6.

If too much heat accumulates, it will be the same as a runner who pushes too hard on a steamy hot day. Eventually, she or he feels weak and faint. The situation can become life threatening if care is not taken to alleviate the affects of overheating. For the engine, the danger is to the internal parts that will fry or at least lightly sauté.

Damage to the engine can take many forms if the excess heat is not removed. When I mentioned earlier that your car's engine generates enough heat to destroy itself, I wasn't kidding. The heat can be so intense that it warps or twists the aluminum or cast-iron cylinder head. It may also burn away the layer of insulation called the head gasket, located between the head and the block. If the cylinder head doesn't sit perfectly straight on the engine block

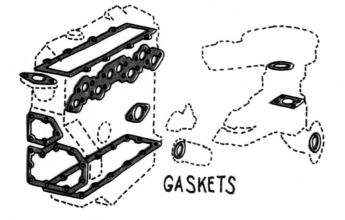

GASKETS

or if the gasket is damaged, the seal that is necessary for proper combustion to take place will be missing. A warped or cracked cylinder head or a blown head gasket will permit the hot combustion gases to escape, resulting in a lack of power and potentially serious engine damage.

As if that weren't enough, internal parts such as pistons and their connecting rods can warp or break. Even the engine block can crack. The noise you would hear before that happens would scare the pants off you, even if the bill for the repairs didn't.

Could it be? Is there an even worse worst possible case? Say it isn't so. The engine can seize—the pistons actually melt into the cylinder walls—never to move again. Once again, you get ample notification with some very loud

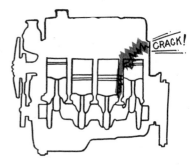

CRACK!

knocking and pounding. The engine? The engine is finito.

No mechanical work is cheap these days, but working on internal engine parts is particularly pricey because it's labor intensive. Hundreds of individual parts make up the engine. Each must be carefully removed and marked so that it can be put back in the right place once reassembly begins. Repairs can cost the equivalent of a couple of days at a plush spa, and I bet you'd rather luxuriate at the spa.

If internal engine work is recommended to you and you don't have a long and happy track record of honest and competent service with the shop or dealership your working with, get a second opinion (as you might for any repairs that are out of the ordinary or seem unusually high priced). Even if your track record is good and long, you may want a second opinion anyway. It is not an insult to a mechanic or shop to take this precautionary measure; it is an accepted and intelligent method of protecting yourself.

More Power

With the advent of the popularity of the 4-cylinder engine as a result of the gas crunch in the 1970s, the V-8 workhorse of the industry and, to a lesser extent, its cousin, the 6-cylinder engine, with their big compression chambers that could pack gobs of gas and air into them and then go lightning fast, were being abandoned for the more fuel-efficient 4-cylinder. For many Americans, the number one priority seemed to be getting from point A to point B using the least amount of gas. Gas hogs were becoming increasingly unpopular. Diesels were popular for a while but never really threatened the gasoline manufactured engine's popularity.

As time has a way of doing, things changed. The gas crisis seemed to disappear, and for many drivers, going fast was once again a priority. The task of automotive engineers became the delivery of more power. But how to do it efficiently and economically? They could return to the larger combustion chambers of the 6- and 8-cylinder engines. But simply enlarging the combustion chambers of most small engines (increasing their displacement) often produces noticeable increases in vibrations. Keeping the cylinder the same size and making it possible for it to eat more of its air/fuel diet quicker is a desirable alternative. Also, smaller engines are more compatible with the popular front wheel drive layout. To accomplish this increased diet, devices were added to engines which pushed more air into the cylinders. Turbochargers, superchargers, and more intake and exhaust valves were added to engines with intercoolers and tuned manifolds. The result was more raw power delivered without sacrificing good gas mileage.

Turbochargers, Superchargers, and Multivalve Engines
Most engines are normally aspirated, that is, they draw the air/fuel mixture into the combustion chambers without assistance. As the piston moves downward in the chamber, it creates a vacuum behind it into which the air/fuel mixture is drawn. It works like a big straw. To get more power out of a normally aspirated engine, it is necessary to force it to breathe in and burn more air and fuel.

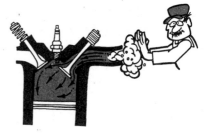

Turbochargers and superchargers force more air and fuel into the combustion chambers of an engine, forcing it to produce more power. A supercharger differs from a turbocharger primarily in the the method it uses to get additional air and fuel into the combustion chambers. The supercharger uses a pump or other device driven by a belt, which works off the power of the running engine's rotating crankshaft. Consequently, it uses some engine power to

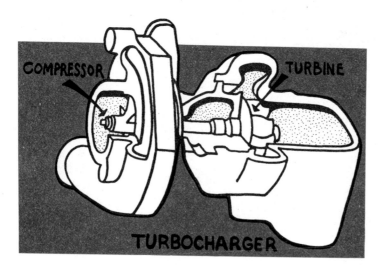

provide it with other power. Instead of a belt, a turbocharger uses some of the excess heat generated by the engine and found in the stream of exhaust gas located in the exhaust manifold. Those hot gases drive a device called a turbine, a word derived from the word *whirlwind* and referring to a spinning thing. A turbine is a machine with 2 sets of blades which spins in oil. When the exhaust gases turn one blade, it turns the other, forcing more air into the engine.

Either a turbocharger or a supercharger can be equipped with an intercooler, a device that, as its name suggests, cools air. Turbochargers and superchargers compress air. Compressing air makes it hotter and less dense. Cooling that same air causes it to become denser. The denser the air, the more air molecules can be packed into the combustion chamber and burned for more power. More air molecules, more diet.

Multivalve engines breathe more air and fuel through additional intake and/or exhaust valves. The more valves an engine has, the more fuel can be burned and the more power generated. A 4-cylinder engine with multi-port fuel injection provides the extra fuel necessary, and extra valves provide four cylinders with the delivery.

The Exhaust System

Your engine would be playing a very noisy concerto, despite its heavy metal outer cover and insulating gaskets, were it not for the muffler. This metal, oblong noise catcher absorbs much of the sound that combustion creates by routing sound waves through its hollow chambers. As important as its job is, it is only one member of a very important team, the exhaust system.

The exhaust system is made up of a series of metal components that are welded together to route burned gases away from the engine and into the atmosphere. It includes the exhaust manifold, a heavy set of cast iron pipes that are attached to the engine, an exhaust pipe that comes in two sections, the header pipe and tail pipe, the catalytic converter, and the muffler. Exhaust systems are often responsible for rattles, roars, knocks, buzzes, and

chatters coming from under the car and noticeable especially at idle. These noises are very often the result of loose parts, fasteners, or hangers that cause the metal components to come in contact with the bottom of the car. Many times, simply retightening the exhaust components will set the system right, but sometimes a piece of metal will have to be bent or rerouted in some way. Most important, faulty exhaust systems can be harmful to your health. If there's a leak anywhere in the system, the exhaust's harmful gases can get sidetracked into the passenger compartment. The entire exhaust system should be checked regularly to ensure that it is operating correctly.

A faulty exhaust can also cause a car to run badly; if it's blocked, the burned gases will not be able to leave the combustion chambers as quickly as they should. Consequently, the new air/fuel mixtures will not be able to enter the combustion chambers as quickly as they should. If this happens, the car will suffer a lack of power.

Emission Controls

Emission controls work hand in hand with the exhaust system in an effort to control the pollution from combustion, which has reached unacceptable proportions throughout this country. Between our cars and our industries, we're doing quite a good job of poisoning the air we breathe. This has taken a visible form in the brown cloud that hangs over many of our cities—the result of increased levels of hydrocarbons and nitrogen oxides. Carbon monoxide emissions, which have also gone beyond acceptable levels, add to the problem despite their invisibility.

Since the early 1960s, the federal government has been attempting to reduce emissions to a safe level by requiring the use of certain devices that control the amount of pollutants engines produce. To describe in depth the emission control components found on most cars today, we would need another book of this size. Instead, here is a simple list of the major devices and a brief description of how they work.

Exhaust Gas Conversion System: This system consists of the catalytic converter which contains special chemicals that turn carbon monoxide and hydrocarbons into such harmless substances as water and carbon dioxide. The catalytic converter is often responsible for lack of power, low gas mileage, and the odor of rotten eggs that occurs from the burning of sulfur in gasolines. It is normal for this odor to occur occasionally, but it *can* be a warning sign of a clogged or defective system. Replacement pellets are available for some catalytic converters, which offer a considerable savings over the cost of a new converter. It's definitely worth asking about if your converter needs replacement. Also included in this system is the oxygen sensor we discussed in chapter 3.

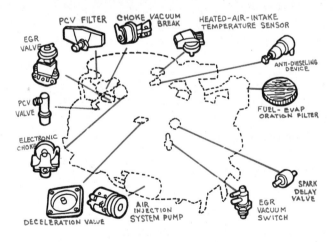

Exhaust Gas Recirculation Systems (EGR): This system, consisting of EGR valve, sensors, solenoid, and switches, recirculates exhaust gases back into the intake manifold where they are burned again. This reduces high combustion temperatures that contribute to pinging. A faulty EGR valve is sometimes the cause of stumbling when the engine is cold, stalling on acceleration and deceleration, hesitating, and rough running. Especially noticeable at idle when the engine is warm are surging and lack of power.

Evaporative Emission Control System: The vapor storage cannister and filter, fuel filter cap, purge valve, and solenoid comprise this sytem. A cannister traps vapors from the fuel tank and carburetor and redirects them to the engine, where they are stored in a charcoal cannister until the engine starts and then burned. If you notice an odor of gasoline in the car, this could be the cause. This system may also be responsible for hard starting and rough idle.

Positive Crankcase Ventilation System (PCV): The PCV valve and solenoid pick up gases that have escaped into the crankcase from the combustion chambers (blowby gases) and return them to the engine for burning. Hard staring, rough idle, power loss, and excessive oil burning are sometimes related to this system's malfunctioning.

Air Injection System: This system, which includes the air pump and antibackfire or deceleration valve, adds oxygen to the exhaust by means of a belt-driven pump that helps burn hydrocarbons. Other valves, including a diverter valve and reed valve, help to make the air/fuel mixture burn leaner by diverting the flow of air from the pump during deceleration.

Heated-Air-Intake System: This system maintains the flow of warm air into the carburetor, which allows for a leaner, more combustible mixture. A faulty intake system may be responsible for stalling, hesitation, pinging, and power loss.

Fuel Metering System: Many of the components on both fuel injection models and models with carburetors have been developed to control emissions. On fuel injection systems, these include the fuel injectors, the electronic control module or computer command module, deceleration controls, and the EFI mixture control unit. On carburetor models, these include mixture settings on sealed carburetors, the mixture control solenoid, the electronic choke, an altitude compensator sensor, feedback control sensors, and the thermostatic air cleaner. In addition, carburetors are

equipped with antidieseling devices to prevent run on
after the engine is shut off.

Your car may have a few or many of the above devices,
and it may have additional devices that are not listed here.
It isn't important that you commit these to memory, but it
is important that you realize that emission control components affect the performance of your car's engine to a great
extent and are often the cause of failed emission tests. Furthermore, when emission control devices malfunction,
they are often the cause of numerous driveability or runa-
bility problems, producing symptoms that are very similar
to those produced by traditional fuel, ignition, and timimg
components. To avoid the replacement of more expensive
fuel and ignition components, whose symptoms may be
exactly the same, emission control components should be
thoroughly checked out. A professional engine analysis
will usually bring the faulty component to light.

The best way for you to keep track of the health of your
emission control components, not to mention the general
health of your car's engine, is to regularly keep track of
your gas mileage. A thirstier car may mean a malfunctioning component.

If your emission control system fails because of a defective part, whether or not the part failure causes your car's
emission's to exceed federal emission standards, the
manufacturer is required by federal law to pay for the
repairs for the first five years or 50,000 miles.

5

Cooling, Heating, and Air Conditioning

A car in the breakdown lane, hood up, engine steaming, driver steaming is a familiar sight if you drive the highways in the summer. It's a scene repeated mile after mile as cars drop out of the highway travel lanes like flies. Is it a crap shoot? When your number's up is your number up? Not really.

Despite the fact that a cooling system failure is now the third most frequent cause of roadside breakdowns, following running out of gas and getting a flat tire, there are many things you can do to lessen your chances of joining the breakdown club. An Engine Temperature or Hot light that goes on or a gauge that starts to move into the red zone is a warning sign asking for a rapid response. Even a well-maintained engine can have its cooling system overtaxed by long traffic tie-ups in hot weather. Or you may have to deal with a broken fan belt, hose, thermostat, or

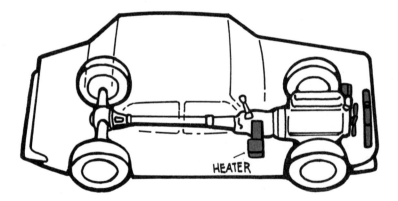

HEATER

water pump at any time. If your car does overheat, there are things you can do to keep the repair bill somewhere below the national deficit and more in the range of a fast food dinner for a family of four.

Today's four-cylinder engines are working harder and handling greater heat than ever before. The explosions taking place inside the engine block which drive the car produce temperatures in excess of 3,500 degrees F—enough heat to melt cast iron, of which, coincidentally, your engine block is probably made. Options such as automatic transmission, power steering, and air conditioning each raise the engine temperature at least 10 degrees.

Your car's engine has an "ideal operating temperature" that permits it to produce maximum power on a minimum diet. So does your body. Both react similarly to change. If your body temperature rises significantly for a prolonged period of time, whether as a consequence of sitting in a hot tub too long or in the hot sun without a hat, damage to the system may result—even death. Similarly, if the temperature of an engine rises beyond a certain point for a significant time, there is a high risk of damaging or destroying the engine. Fortunately, your car is equipped with a cooling system, which in combination with engine oil (we'll talk more about oil in chap. 6), maintains the correct temperature range to help prevent heat stroke.

Most cars are water-cooled. For these the cooling system depends on the flow of liquid in and around the engine. There are, however, a few air-cooled engines, which depend solely on the flow of air in and around the engine.

The Cooling System

Coolant is actually a combination of water and antifreeze, a weird-looking chemical known as ethylene glycol, which you buy in the plastic gallon-size containers. When mixed with water, ethylene glycol keeps the water in your radiator from boiling in summer and freezing in winter. From now on, when I say "coolant," I'll be talking about the mixture of ethylene glycol and water, and when I use the term "antifreeze," I'll be talking about the chemical, ethylene

50%
ANTIFREEZE

50%
H_2O

glycol. The liquid in your car's radiator should always—
365 days a year—be coolant.

Does this mean you shouldn't use straight antifreeze?
Exactly. This is not a case of if a little's good, a lot's better.
Water is not only a better conductor of heat than ethylene
glycol but it is also a necessary catalyst: without it, the
antifreeze doesn't work as it should. If the coolant is more
than 70 percent antifreeze, the antifreeze and its additives,
such as rust inhibitors, stop working. For the coolant system to live a long and healthy life, these additives have to
remain active. Later on, I'll explain why they're such an
important part of the system.

The right proportion of water to antifreeze for your car
can be found—you guessed it—in your owner's manual. It
is this proportion that relates to the coolant's range of temperature protection. Often it's a 50:50 ratio, which will protect an engine from freezing down to -34 degrees F and
raise its boiling point (the water will not boil as quickly)
from 226 to 263 degrees. If you live in Deadhorse, Alaska,
it could be as high as 70:30, which will protect an engine
down to -84 degrees F and raise its boiling point to 274
degrees F. Beyond a 70 percent concentrate of antifreeze,
things start to go downhill rapidly: the protective qualities
of the solution soon disappear.

The coolant is stored in the radiator, which consists of
a metal tank called a core and many narrow metal tubes

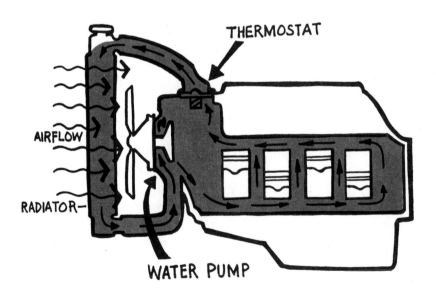

with thin extensions called fins attached to them. A radiator cap seals the system and puts it under 14 to 18 pounds of pressure per square inch. When the engine is running, a water pump that is powered by a belt attached to the turning engine draws coolant out of the radiator and into the engine compartment through the lower radiator hose. From there, it travels through copper-lined passageways that surround the cylinders in a sleeve called a water jacket. As the coolant travels around each cylinder, it picks up much of the excess heat. The now-warm fluid then flows back toward the radiator via the upper radiator hose where it passes through a one-way, heat sensitive door called a thermostat—if the temperature is correct.

Yes, this is the most notorious of all the small parts for your car. Until the coolant reaches a predetermined temperature (180-205 degrees), the thermostat remains closed, blocking the flow of coolant and forcing it to recirculate around each of the hot combustion chambers. When the coolant finally does reach a predetermined temperature, the thermostat door opens and the coolant flows out through the upper radiator hose into the radiator. It then dribbles down through the finned tubes where most of the heat is released into the air.

If the car is moving, it is the normal flow of outside air that dissipates the heat, which is why radiators are always positioned in the front of the engine. When a car is at rest, nature is not so helpful, and a fan that is run, either by a rubber belt or a thermostat (the kind you have on the dining room wall), pulls cool air from the outside through the radiator, thus releasing most of the heat. By the time the coolant reaches the lower portion of the radiator, it's cool enough to repeat the journey through the lower radiator hose and ready to do its job all over again.

Assuming the correct level and proportion of coolant are maintained, and the water pump, thermostat, fan, and radiator cap are in working order, the correct temperature for the engine will be achieved and you and your car, happy as clams, can drive merrily on. All it takes is a little TLC to make this driving dream a reality.

Every other time you buy gas, or as often as each week during the summer, check to be sure there is plenty of coolant. Most cars today have an overflow reservoir, a translucent plastic container located near the radiator and attached to it by a narrow rubber hose. These overflow reservoirs make this maintenance check a breeze. Without even removing the cap, you can see whether the coolant is at the FULL line. There will probably be two lines, one for when the engine's cold and one for when it's hot. If the coolant level is below the appropriate line, wait until the engine is cold, remove the cap on the reservoir, and add the mixture of antifreeze and water recommended in your owner's manual.

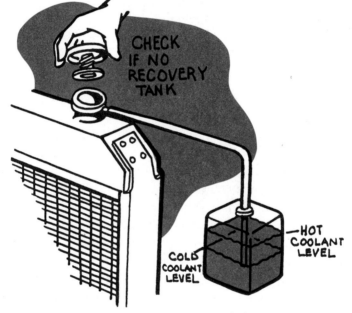

If your car doesn't have an overflow reservoir, remove the radiator cap, again when the engine is cold, and look inside. Most radiators caps have either a safety release valve or a safety catch. The release lever lets the pressure in the cooling system release gradually. The catch is designed to hold the cap in place even if additional pressure is still in the system. To remove a radiator cap, take a rag from your emergency kit, place it over the cap, turn your face away from the radiator, and turn it ¼ of a turn

CAUTION: Don't even think about opening a radiator cap or overflow reservoir if the engine is hot.

and stop. Only when all pressure has been released should you turn it the rest of the way and remove it. The coolant should reach within 1 or 2 inches of the top of the radiator, and no fins should be visible.

As with all your car's fluids, you want to be aware of changes in fluid consumption. But if you are checking regularly and you are constantly replacing large amounts of coolant, have the system looked at by a professional. Leaks don't always show up on your garage floor or in your driveway. Some leaks only occur when the engine is under the higher pressures of highway driving. The amount of coolant that is right for your car can also be found in your owner's manual under "Liquid Capacity." It could be four gallons or five or six, depending on the size of the engine.

Use only antifreeze that is suitable for all engine types, including aluminum (this will be indicated on the label). Part of the engine—the cylinder head and, in a few cars, even the engine block—may be made of lightweight aluminum rather than cast iron. Aluminum is susceptible to certain corrosive elements. Only antifreeze that states on the label "Suitable for all engine types, including aluminum" contains the special additives that protect all types of engine metals.

Each year, get a professional maintenance check of the entire coolant system. The radiator, water pump, fan, thermostat(s), radiator cap, and fluid should all be examined to be sure they are in good condition. At this time, all belts, hoses, and clamps should also be checked. A loose or broken fan or water pump belt can be responsible for overheating, with serious and expensive engine damage as the inevitable consequence. Any belt or hose that appears brittle, flaky, cracked, or mushy should be replaced at this time.

CHECKING ANTIFREEZE CONCENTRATION

Coolant should be clear and look like it just came from the Blue Grotto, not the Black Lagoon. If it resembles the latter, it's time to get the system drained and flushed by a professional. This is where the additives previously referred to come into play. Over time, the coolant system corrodes and rust forms inside. The rust accumulates in deposits that eventually clog the passageways and prevent the flow of coolant. You may not even get a warning in the way of a flashing TEMP light or gauge that moves out of

the normal zone if the cylinder that is deprived of the coolant is too far away from the temperature warning sensor
to pick up the problem. That cylinder, deprived of the cooling liquid, will fry.

To play it safe, have the coolant system drained and
flushed every two to three years or whenever your owner's
manual recommends. All coolant loses its protective qualities eventually. The old coolant should be removed and a
liquid solvent designed to remove rust should be circulated
through the entire system to make sure all the passageways are open. The system is then refilled with the proper
amount and proportion of coolant. Before arranging with a
professional to have this work done, be sure you know
exactly what is included in each price you obtain.

When All Else Fails

Even a well-maintained system can be overtaxed by long
traffic tie-ups in hot weather. If you see your engine TEMP
light go on and stay on or the temperature gauge needle
begins to move out of the normal zone, there are several
things you can do. First, turn off the air conditioning; it
makes the engine work 20 percent harder and therefore
hotter. Then, turn your car's heater to its highest setting
and put on the blower, which will pull some of the heat
away from the engine and into the passenger compartment. This might be a good time to open the windows. Of
course, now you will overheat, but remember, dry cleaning
your suit is cheaper than rebuilding your engine.

Try to increase the distance between you and the car
directly in front of you. Its tail pipe is sending out hot
exhaust fumes that are making a bad problem worse. This

may be trickier than it sounds if the driver behind you, having majored in obnoxious behavior, has grafted his front bumper onto your rear bumper in the belief that every inch of forward movement is going to make a difference in reaching his destination on time. So take this last action with caution.

If your car has a fan driven by a belt not controlled by a thermostat (this is probably not the time to try to figure this out), put the car in Neutral and gently rev the engine by lightly pressing on the accelerator pedal a few times. Doing this will bring more air into the system and may help cool things down a bit. If it's hot enough to stir-fry on the pavement, this strategy may not help.

If all else fails and your car is still overheating, it's time to turn your hazard lights on, get the car safely off the road, and turn the engine off. Lift the hood and wait until the engine is thoroughly cool (a minimum of 30 minutes). Only then should you begin to look for the cause of the overheating. First, check the level of the coolant by observing the coolant reservoir or removing the radiator cap. **Never open the coolant reservoir or remove the radiator cap until you are absolutely certain the engine is cold.** By placing the coolant under 14 to 18 pounds of pressure, the radiator cap raises the boiling point of the coolant. If the cap is removed and the pressure released, the coolant could immediately boil. It could burst out of the radiator and the escaping steam could injure you. If the coolant level is down, you will have to add some from the container you always keep in the trunk. Right? Right.

If water is all that is available, it is better than nothing. Remember that water will boil before coolant would have, so drive to a service station as soon as possible to have the radiator drained and the proper coolant mixture added. Add hot water when possible. Adding cold water can be like putting a very cold plate in a very hot oven, something's likely to give, and you don't want that to be your engine block.

Next check the radiator hoses for leaks. Do not check hoses by squeezing them while they are hot. A weakened hose could collapse, allowing scalding hot coolant to spray out. Check the belt for the water pump and, if there is one, for the fan. The belt may be loose or it may have broken and be missing entirely. Now is when that backup bag of saved belts is going to look like a winning 50-1 shot at the races.

CAUTION: No two emergency situations are alike. Your concern for your personal safety must guide your response.

Continuing to drive a car that is overheating could cost you a ruined engine and a big labor bill for repair or replacement. Never let the needle on your engine temperature gauge reach the danger (red) zone or let the TEMP light stay on for more than 30 seconds as permanent damage to the working parts of the engine is practically inevitable. Don't turn an inconvenience into an economic disaster.

Important Facts about Hot Weather Driving

Slow-moving traffic in summer can cause even the healthiest car to overheat occasionally, especially the smaller four-cylinder ones that produce 20 percent more heat than their six or eight-cylinder relatives. If, after letting the system cool down, you check and find nothing apparently wrong, it is normally safe to drive the car, assuming the coolant level indicator is working correctly. You may not even need to consult a mechanic.

Like a jogger in the summertime who runs too many miles or completes a particularly strenuous course on an especially hot day and experiences heat exhaustion, your car may sometimes need to rest in the shade and get its fluid balance back. Listen to your body and your car. Respond by giving each system a rest and replacing lost fluids before returning to a normal routine.

Should the car continue to overheat, you probably have

a more serious problem, such as a broken water pump, a leaky radiator, a cracked hose, or a bum thermostat. If your car is suffering from mechanical heatstroke, proceed to a service station, but stop the car as soon as the engine TEMP light comes on again or the needle on the engine temperature gauge starts to creep into the danger zone. Let the engine cool down again. If the station is very far away, this may be a painfully long process. It takes patience, but if you don't spend the time, you will spend the money. Driver's choice.

Overheating problems that are the result of more serious damage, such as a blown head gasket or warped or cracked cylinder head or engine block, can be tough to detect. While most external leaks will show up using a simple pressure tester, internal leaks take skill, patience, and the right diagnostic equipment. Most good radiator shops will have a dye test to locate hard to find leaks. If that doesn't uncover the problem, they can analyze the radiator's emissions. An internal leak will often draw coolant into the combustion chamber where it is then burned with the exhaust gases. Sometimes it shows up in the form of coolant in the engine oil or transmission fluid, which you may see as white steamy smoke coming from the tail pipe. (Don't confuse this with the normal exhaust color of tail pipe emissions on a cold day.) Exhaust gases often appear in the radiator. An exhaust gas emissions analyzer and a combustion leak tester are devices used to determine the presence of these exhaust gases in the radiator steam.

In an ideal world, the proper maintenance of the cooling system would keep you from ever facing these tricky and expensive engine problems. But this is not an ideal world. If the system does fail and there is serious damage to the engine, remember to get a second opinion before jumping into major overhaul and repairs. Unless you know and would trust the shop with your firstborn, a second opinion is the best way to limit your chances of being ripped off.

There is one organization of radiator shops, the National Automotive Radiator Service Association (NARSA), that I'm aware of (there may be others) which monitors its members to ensure that they are trained with the most current technical information. If you find a shop that is a member, it would be a good place to start to find competent help for a tricky overheating problem. But as is the case with any repair shop's membership in a trade organization, consider it just the first step in assuring yourself of fair treatment. Checking out their references before you bring them your car, as you would any business that provides you with a service, is mandatory.

Does It Matter If an Engine Runs Cold?

You bet it does. And the consequences, while they may not be as initially damaging as an engine that runs too hot, are serious. We talked about ideal engine temperatures and how important they are in helping to burn off the deposits of combustion that cause premature engine wear. Sludge loves engines that never reach their ideal temperatures. It gives this fiend a chance to multiply with impunity. There are a number of reasons for overcooling. Two of the most common causes are a broken thermostat that never closes (and so never warms the coolant adequately) and a low coolant level. In addition to the lack of heat that you will notice when you turn the heat on, there will be a noticeable drop in gas mileage. Overcooled engines are gas guzzlers.

The Heating System

Did you ever wonder why on a cold day it seems to take forever to get the windshield and you defrosted? Blame the cooling system, not the heater, for it is the coolant that actually warms you. If the system is working properly,

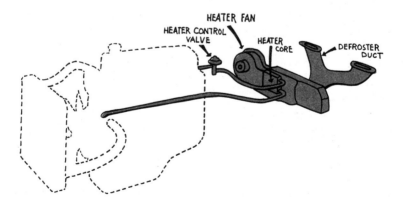

when you turn the heater/defroster button or lever on in your car, heated coolant is diverted from its normal journey. Instead of flowing from the engine block where it was warmed to the radiator where most of its heat would have been dissipated, the coolant is drawn to a smaller radiator, the heater core, located directly in front of the passenger compartment. A fan, which is run by a blower motor (a simple electrical motor), forces the warmth of the coolant out of the heater core, past a valve, and into the air that is blown through ducts or passageways leading into the passenger compartment. This warm air circulates and keeps you warm even when the temperature outside is freezing.

The amount of heat flowing into the passenger compartment is determined by the volume of coolant that is directed through the heater core and the amount of outside air that is let in through the grille at the base of the windshield to regulate that heat. When you turn the heater on, you permit the coolant to flow through the heater core. When you set the different heater and defroster controls, you open and close vents leading inside the car, directing the heat to different places in the passenger compartment—up to the windshield, down to the passengers. A thermostat may also control these vents, in which case they will open and close automatically in response to a heat sensor.

Problems in the heating system that can usually be identified relatively easily include a plugged heater core, a stuck vent, a broken or worn blower motor, a leak in the heater core, or a kinked hose. Windshield fogging when you turn the defroster on or a wet passenger carpet are symptoms of a leaky heater core, and a kinked hose will often notify you with a low moaning sound. But the most common problem (and the cheapest to fix) is air in the system. The overwhelming majority of all heater problems could be remedied by simply bleeding (removing) air from the system. If your heating system isn't working properly, and there isn't an obvious cause, be sure that the system is thoroughly bled before anything more exotic and expensive is tried.

Air conditioning, whether it's in your car or your house, works like a refrigerator. Just think of yourself as a frozen dinner the next time you turn yours on. Air conditioning is based on two principles: (1) when any liquid becomes a vapor or gas, it absorbs heat, and conversely, when a vapor becomes a liquid, it gives off heat; and (2) heat always moves from a warmer spot to a cooler spot. Air conditioning doesn't add cold, it removes heat; it removes heat from one area and sends it to another area through the use of a fluid called refrigerant.

Known as both R-12 and Freon, refrigerant is the medium for exchanging heat and cold. From now on, I will refer to refrigerant as Freon. Freon boils at -21 degrees F, a temperature at which most other liquids freeze. This unique property is about to come in very handy.

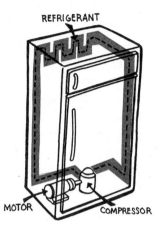

When the engine is running and the air conditioning is turned on, the following process takes place. Although individual components may vary from car to car, the following basics apply to all air conditioning systems. Within a sealed system, Freon is circulated through an evaporator or series of coils located under the firewall in the passenger compartment. An expansion valve (another one-way door) regulates the flow of Freon into the evaporator. As the Freon moves through the evaporator, it boils, and the first basic principle of air conditioning takes over: as the Freon turns from a liquid to a gas, it absorbs the heat from inside the car.

From the evaporator, the Freon, full of its newly acquired heat, moves to the compressor, a pump that is driven by a belt attached to the crankshaft. Just as it would seem, the compressor compresses the gas under extremely high pressure.

From the compressor, the Freon goes to the condenser, which looks like a radiator and sits in front of the regular radiator. In the condenser, the compressor's high pressurizing dramatically raises the temperature of the Freon to over 150 degrees F. In the fins of the condenser, air from the outside is now passed over the Freon. The Freon cools and returns to a liquid state. Just as it absorbed heat when

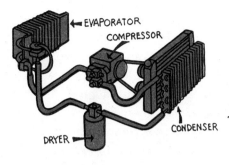

it turned into a gas, now it gives up its heat as it turns from a gas to a liquid.

As a high pressure liquid once again, the Freon flows to the receiver dryer, which is a kind of filter. The receiver separates any remaining gas from the liquid and removes any moisture through the use of either calcium oxide or sulfuric acid—both chemicals that are attracted to water. Air conditioning units hate moisture.

If you notice a small puddle of liquid on the ground under the area of the radiator on a hot day, it usually means that excess moisture has been removed by the air conditioning process. But be sure it's water and not another vital liquid spewing out of a nearby spot.

The liquid Freon, free of moisture, passes back inside the passenger compartment to the evaporator. On its way, an expansion valve regulates the amount of liquid that flows into the evaporator. The liquid is now under low pressure and is again about to boil, absorbing the heat and cooling the air inside the car. A blower motor forces this cooled air into the car through flaps. This process of going from a liquid to a vapor absorbing and releasing heat is what cools the inside of our cars, our homes, and our refrigerators.

For Professionals Only

To operate properly, the air conditioning system must have the correct amount of Freon. This amount is specific to your car and needs to be recharged periodically. Look in your owner's manual for the correct interval. Recharging takes a competent professional.

The air conditioning system is a particularly dangerous one for amateur tinkering. The Freon boils at a very low temperature. If it comes in contact with the skin, it will burn it easily. In contact with a flame or other heat source, it can change into a poisonous gas. Add too much Freon and it can explode. This is a job for a professional.

In addition, all air conditioning components— compressor, evaporator, condenser, receiver, blower motor, and expansion valve—must be in good working order. The receiver, which has a peephole for detecting problems, must be operating correctly. The compressor and the belt that drives it must be healthy and have the right tension. The compressor also has a magnetic clutch that allows it to turn on and off as needed. As with any electrical component, before letting anyone replace a compressor, make sure they check the fuse and the electrical ground. (For more about grounds, see chap. 7.) The same is true for the blower motor; its fan and electrical wiring must be working properly in order for the cool air to be circulated throughout the passenger compartment.

The best thing you can do to keep your air conditioning in healthy working order is to run the system once a week whenever the outside temperature is above 50 degrees F. The many rubber seals that join different components of this system will dry and crack if not lubricated by the oil that is added to the system and that circulates with the Freon. It only lubricates when the air conditioning is on.

In fact, a good way to detect leaks in the air conditioning (usually found at joints or couplings) is by the presence of dried compressor oil. Leaking Freon evaporates immediately in the air and so leaves no telltale trace. It is the dried lubricating oil on any of the air conditioning components or hoses (except sometimes the compressor itself that is the only clue. Leaks should be fixed by a professional.

If you don't run the air conditioning regularly, you may hear a loud squeaking when you finally do. This is generally nothing to worry about. The compressor seals gradually sag and will normally protest with a good squeak until they return to normal shape after a short period of use.

6

Oil

Oil is a jack-of-all-trades. It lubricates, it cleans, and in combination with the cooling system, it cools. Oil is the lifeblood of your car's engine, and like the blood that circulates through your body, it must be of a certain quality and in sufficient quantity to supply all its dependent parts adequately. Cut off the circulation because the fluid is too thick or too thin, or because a passageway is restricted, or because there is a leak somewhere in the system, and it won't be long before damage, often irreparable, is done. Without oil, your engine's a goner.

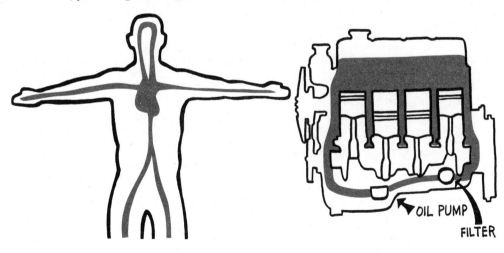

Oil Cleans, Cools, and Lubricates

When the car is not in use, most of the oil sits in a metal pan attached to the bottom of the engine block. As the ignition key is turned on, an oil pump located at the bottom of the pan pressurizes the oil and forces it through a strainer and then through an oil filter, where dirt and contaminants, the natural by-products of combustion, are caught and stored until the filter is changed.

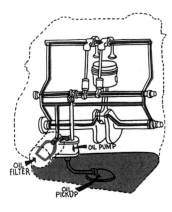

From the filter, the oil is pushed up into the main gallery, an enclosed passageway with smaller passageways leading from it. Oil moves to the bearings, connecting rods, and inside the cylinder walls, pistons, and valves, where it acts as a lubricant: it coats the parts with a thin film of liquid that provides a slippery cushion for the rapidly moving parts. The oil is forced to the valve train where it provides a slippery surface for the valves to slide up and down within their sleeves. Without this protective film, the bearings, pistons, valves, and other internal parts would be in direct contact with each other—a destructive situation. **Metal against metal causes friction; friction causes heat; and heat causes wear.** Wear translates into premature engine wear and expensive repairs.

And that's just the beginning. At the same time the oil is separating pistons from cylinders and other moving parts, it is circulating around each of the cylinders. Since it is a reasonably good conductor of heat, the oil picks up much of the excess as it flows around the hot combustion chambers and carries that heat to the oil pan below. This clever design works like clockwork if (1) the oil is at the proper level; (2) the oil is clean and of the correct weight and type; (3) the filter and pump are working properly; and (4) the passageways are clear and do not inhibit the oil flow.

For years, the same service station attendant who pumped gas into our car was kind enough to check the oil level for us. "Check your oil, ma'am?" was heard as frequently as "And away we go." The only thing we had to do

was extend our wallet. Since the mid-1970s, however, the number of full-service gas stations has dropped dramatically. Instead of "Check your oil?" we now hear "I can't come out of the booth"—and they mean it.

If you patronize a station that performs full service, and you're willing to pay, great. But like it or not, our self-serve world is growing. (I can't wait until they have me check out my own groceries.) We as consumers have no choice, unless we want to buy the "higher priced spread," but to perform more and more of our own routine maintenance checks. If we ignore these periodic checks (oil, coolant, transmission, power steering, brakes, and windshield wiper solutions), we'll be the ones who suffer the consequences: premature wear of engine parts, damaged engines, large and unnecessary repair bills, and reduced safety.

How and When to Check Oil

For oil, that means checking the level every other time you buy gas. Even if someone else is doing the routine maintenance on your car, it still pays to know how to check your car's fluid levels, if only for emergency purposes. Even the best-maintained cars can develop problems. The oil light on the dashboard may come on and stay on for more than 20 seconds or the oil gauge needle move out of the safe range while you're driving, and there may be no one else around to check the dipstick. If no oil shows on the stick and the car is driven, the engine will probably suffer damage. If you don't know what the dipstick looks like when the oil pan is full, you're not going to know what it looks like when the level is dangerously low. And you're not going to be in a position to make a sound decision about whether or not you should continue driving the car.

Check the oil level in the morning, when the engine is cold. Once the engine has been turned on, you have to wait at least five minutes for the oil to drain back into the pan to get an accurate reading. If you check immediately after you stop the engine, a fair amount of the oil will remain where it's been—inside the cylinders and oil galleries. Less oil will show on the dipstick than is actually present in the engine. As you can imagine, standing around at a busy self-serve pump waiting for the oil to drain for five minutes may require that you beef up your life insurance.

With the car parked on level ground, locate the dipstick. This can be a tougher job than it would appear if the dipstick (and this is not uncommon) has been cleverly disguised as the transmission dipstick, or just cleverly disguised.

Now, pull it out and wipe a clean cloth down its entire length: look at the marks and the words on the stick. Once it has oil all over it, it will be much harder to read. Not all dipsticks are the same, since there is no uniformity in the industry. There will, however, always be two marks that indicate the high and low levels for a particular engine. Your owner's manual should illustrate the dipstick for your car. If you don't find it there, ask your mechanic to break the code for you. Don't assume that there's anything wrong with you because you're having trouble either locating it or reading it. Until recently, making fluid checks easy and their containers accessible was not a high priority for most manufacturers. For some manufacturers, it would appear that it is still not a priority.

Put the stick back in, as close to the angle at which it came out as possible. Pull it out again and this time notice where the oil film lies on the stick. If the film is below the add line, then put in a quart of the same weight (number) as is already in the engine. Recheck the stick. Be sure to wipe the stick thoroughly before using it to recheck the level, otherwise you won't get a true reading.

If the level reads between the add and full lines, should you add another full quart? No! If there is too much oil in the pan, the engine seals, which make certain no oil escapes through the joints, may burst, leaving you with an oil leak. Too much oil also raises the level to the point where the crankshaft actually rests in it. As the crankshaft turns, it whips the oil, adding air to it, just as an egg beater would. The oil will have the consistency of egg whites. Airy. Great for meringues. No good for engines.

Airy oil loses its "stickability." Even though it will reach the cylinder walls in sufficient quantity, it won't stay there. For those of you who cook, it's like a bearnaise sauce: when it's just right, the sauce coats the metal spoon. (I only know about this from reading cookbooks—the only thing my béarnaise sauce ever coats is the inside of the kitchen sink. That's where the runny mess lands after I tell my guests that we're avoiding rich foods.)

If the dipstick is reading significantly more than full, have it checked by a professional whose judgment you trust. Have the pan drained to the proper level if necessary. Your engine will live longer.

If you want to "top off" your oil by adding half a quart when the dipstick shows that it is down only half a quart, that's fine, although some four-cylinder engines actually like running a little short of the full mark. All engines, unless the owner's manual says otherwise, are designed to run safely with the oil level at the add line, but not below. Since many oil containers are now resealable, adding less than a quart and storing the remainder is practical.

Engines vary enormously in the rate they consume oil. One car may use a quart every 500 miles while another uses a quart every 3,500 miles. Even cars that are the same make, model, and year consume oil differently. In addition, oil consumption changes under different driving conditions; for example, oil consumption increases at high speeds. The key is to keep track of what your engine uses. Only if you notice a significant change in oil consumption in combination with normal use should you be concerned. If this does occur, just like any similar change in your car's consumption of fluids, have a professional look at it.

What to Do If the Oil Light Comes On

If the oil light comes on and stays on for more than 20 seconds, or the oil pressure gauge moves out of the proper range, find a safe place to pull over, stop the car, and turn off the engine. Unless the dashboard light's wiring is malfunctioning or the sending unit is faulty, the light is trying to tell you that the engine oil is not circulating properly. This is not a "By the way, next time you're in for service, let's have a look" light. An engine without oil creates a serious, inconvenient, and potentially expensive situation that demands immediate attention.

After you have found a safe place to stop the car and a quick check reveals no oil on the dipstick, do not drive the car except to provide for your own safety. A car driven when no oil shows on the dipstick, for whatever reason, can be damaged in very little time. The repair bill can be very big time.

It may be that the oil level is too low, either because the burned oil has not been replaced routinely or because there's a leak in the system. Like other leaks, an oil leak will not necessarily show up in your driveway. Some only occur as a result of the greater stress of highway driving. A seal may have broken, and all the oil may have silently poured out onto the highway as you were driving along.

It could be that the oil pump is worn or broken and is no longer pressurizing the oil. If that happens, regardless of how much oil is in the pan, it won't circulate properly. The oil won't reach and lubricate the rapidly moving internal parts—friction, heat, and wear will result.

An oil light could come on out of simple neglect. Oil should be clear. It can be colored amber or reddish, depending on what the manufacturer uses for additives, but it should not be black and full of flotsam and jetsam. Sludge, the unburned deposits that form as the engine runs, discolor the oil and eventually thicken and coat the inner parts of the engine, causing them to work harder and wear faster. If the oil is not changed regularly, eventually these deposits clog the oil passageways. Consequently, despite an adequate supply in the oil pan, oil won't circulate through the passageways properly and possibly not at all. The cylinders and valve train parts will rapidly wear away because precious oil is not reaching them, lubricating them, and redistributing the excess heat as it should.

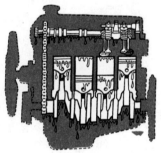

The human body is analogous. Consider a person whose lifetime diet contains large amounts of cholesterol. Eventually, the arteries become clogged and serious health problems arise due to the blood's inability to flow properly through the life-supporting veins and arteries. Oil keeps combustion contaminants in suspension. When the oil is changed, the deposits are removed, and new oil is added to continue doing the same job. If new oil is not added at the appropriate time, the deposits get to do their dirty work. While it may be possible to clean a neglected engine by pumping cleaners through it to remove the deposits, very often the only cure is the far more expensive one of disassembling the entire engine and cleaning the parts and passageways. This costly job, on an engine that has already had abnormal wear, should never have to be done if the oil has been changed regularly from the first.

If you want to keep your car and get the maximum mileage out of it without putting money into engine repairs, you should have the oil changed every spring, summer, winter, and fall. Have it changed every 5,000 miles if

you're a traveling salesperson and only encounter three stoplights a year (normal service in your maintenance schedule), or every 3,500 miles or less if you're like the rest of us who do a lot of stop-and-go driving. This second category is called severe service in your owner's manual despite the fact it's the way most of us drive.

Replace the filter when you have the oil changed. Just as with any of the car's filters, for example, the one in the air cleaner, once a filter is full it can no longer store dirt and contaminants. An oil filter has a special door, a bypass

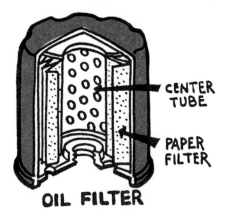

OIL FILTER

valve. Once the filter is full, this valve allows the dirt and contaminants to bypass the filter and go directly to the working parts. Since there's no way to see into the filter (and once it's removed it generally should not be reused), you would need to be clairvoyant to know for sure when the filter is full.

I realize that this may represent a significant investment over a 12-month period, but if you want to keep your car healthy and get the maximum mileage out of it without major repairs, the single smartest thing you can do is change the oil and the filter every season. This expense is an investment in your car's long-term future as well as your bank book. Even if you don't plan to own your car for many years, changing the oil and filter often and keeping an accurate record may increase the car's resale value.

The Right Weight Oil

Oil is designated by two different criteria. One is the weight of the oil. This refers to the oil's viscosity—its ability to flow at different temperatures—and is given by a range of numbers (5-50, thin to thick). The other criterion identifies the composition, that is, what additives went into it and how they will hold up under stress and wear. The use of the letters SC, SD, SE, SF, and SG for gasoline engines and CB, CC, and CD for diesel engines indicates the composition.

Because oil is as essential to an engine's health and well-being as blood is to our body's health, it must perform correctly. It has to flow easily enough to get up inside the cylinder walls and passageways. It must do this very quickly after the engine begins running; otherwise, the parts are moving, but they're not protected by fluid as they need to be. Most engine wear occurs within the first few moments after the car is started.

If oil of an incorrect weight has been added, for example, too heavy, it may not be reaching the internal parts. I learned this firsthand. I was still working at the body shop and also traveling with my seminars. Prior to taking off on a long trip, I went to the shop to change the oil in my car. It was late, I was in a hurry, and I grabbed what I believed was the correct weight oil for my car, 10W 30. Confidently, I poured it in and took off on my trip—a practice I don't recommend. Give yourself a day or two around town before you leave after any maintenance or repairs, just in case anything goes wrong. To continue, about 30 minutes into my drive, the oil light came on. Dumbfounded, I stopped the car, checked the stick, and it read full. Assuming the pump was not working properly, I let the car cool down and drove at a moderate speed to the nearest service station, carefully watching that the oil light did not come on again.

As it turned out, I had mistakenly added a thick 50 weight oil that we kept around for one of the "antique" cars that decorated the shop. This car had many, many miles on it and its internal parts were badly worn, causing it to burn lots of oil. Rather than overhaul the engine, the owner of the shop had added a heavier weight oil, which helped seal the combustion chambers and compensated to some degree for the wear. It worked fine for the antique, but my little car's internal parts were not worn and required a much lighter weight oil for proper circulation. It was a classic case of what's good for the goose is not good for the gander.

Oil and Temperature Change

Oil is sensitive to temperature fluctuations. Its consistency changes in response to the outside temperatures.

Cold temperatures cause the oil to go from the consistency of cooking oil to that of honey. In the honey state, it may not reach the rapidly moving internal parts in time to coat them in fluid and protect them from wear.

Warm temperatures cause the oil to thin out. It goes from the consistency of cooking oil to that of vinegar. The oil can't coat and separate the moving parts, because it doesn't remain on them long enough. Too thick or too thin, the oil won't function as it must to protect your engine.

For many years, the answer to temperature fluctuations was to change the weight of the oil in summer and in winter. As the temperature dropped, you might change from the normal weight oil for your car to a thinner one

(from 10W 40 to 10W 30). The lower the number, the thinner the oil. The thin oil was replaced with a thicker one as the temperature rose. If you lived in an area with little variability in seasonal temperatures, you could sometimes use the same weight oil all year.

As petroleum product technology developed, multigrade oils were developed. Additives called "viscosity index improvers" were included in the oil to extend its working range. Like a singer who with training can increase the effective range of her voice, viscosity improvers gave oil the qualities of more than one grade of oil. These multigrade oils flow correctly when it's hot and when it's cold, thus eliminating the need to change to a different weight oil according to the season.

In recent years, car manufacturers have discouraged the use of oils with a wide range of additives. A 10W 40 oil will flow properly at a wider range of temperatures than a 10W 30 oil but has more additives. The suspicion is that the additives break down, coat the engine's internal parts, and cause them to wear prematurely. It is preferable to use an oil with as narrow a temperature range as possible, while still protecting the engine, and not have to change seasonally.

Check your owner's manual for the exact recommendation regarding oil weight. **Red Alert: By using the incorrect oil, you may waive warranty protection.** Let's say you use 10W 30 weight oil in your engine and the manufacturer's recommendation is for 10W 40. A problem later arises that can be traced to the weight of the oil. The manufacturer may have the right to deny warranty coverage.

Unfair, you say? Not really. The problem is that engines are designed these days to withstand great heat, vigorous movement, and enormous pressures—pressures that reach thousands of pounds per square inch! Consequently, engines are extremely sensitive to the different fluids that they need to survive. Quite simply, they do not function the way they should when the proper replacement fluids are not used. Different systems have different needs, in nature (the calories required by one person to make it through the day are dramatically different from those of another) and in cars.

How to Choose Quality Oil

How about quality? Do you have to buy the most expensive brand to get the best protection? This is where the letters SC-SG and CB-CD are important. The quality of oil is determined by its additives and how it holds up to pressure and wear. Each manufacturer puts different combinations of additives into its oil, including detergents, deoxidizers, rust inhibitors, foam reducers, and various other things designed to improve performance and battle the many enemies that try to reduce engine life.

The American Petroleum Institute (API) and the Society of Automotive Engineers (SAE) have established certain standards of performance for oils. Manufacturers have to submit test results of their products to get API and SAE approval and receive a letter rating. The letters refer to the way the oil meets new car warranty standards for the specific year in which the car was manufactured. For example, SD is suitable for the majority of gasoline engines manufactured from 1968 to 1970, SE for 1972-1979 cars, and SF for 1980-1988 cars. The ratings go from SC-SG for gasoline engines and CA-CD for diesel engines. Beginning in 1989, most new gasoline engines will require SG and CD, respectively. SG has improved antiwear additives to meet the needs of the current generation of high pressure, high power engines.

Motor oils should also contain high detergent additives. This reference will often appear on the can as HD. What is important is that you use the weight recommended in your owner's manual and that the oil meets "new car warranty standards." It should say so on the label.

About Synthetic Oils

Beginning with Mobil I, petroleum producers have been making engine oils from a synthetic or nonpetroleum base. Up to this time, engine oils had been made by refining or purifying petroleum, the dark oozy liquid that flows out of the earth when it is broken into and tapped. Scientists theorize that petroleum is the compressed remains of entire plant and animal civilizations long since buried and preserved in a specific state of decomposition.

Synthetic oils can do things that petroleum-based oils cannot, but they are considerably more expensive. The question is, do you need the things they can do? Synthetics are especially suitable for extremely cold climates or unusual wear. Their ability to flow at very low temperatures is part of the reason, but they also resist breaking down or "shearing" under hard use.

As an oil cools and warms in response to changes in engine temperature, it begins to lose both additives and consistency. Synthetics are more shear stable, that is, they resist that breakdown to a greater degree. If you choose to use them for the benefits they offer, don't follow the manufacturer's recommended change intervals. Your automobile warranty may be voided if you don't follow its recommended intervals.

What about specialty oils for turbochargers and super-chargers? Oils produced for use in turbocharged and super-charged engines are specifically designed to deal with the tremendous heat that develops within the turbocharger or supercharger (see chap. 4 for more about chargers) and remains after the engine is turned off. The carbon deposits that are formed while the engine cools down may coat the bearings and cause them to wear away at a fast and expensive rate. The special oils, including synthetics, designed with these high temperatures in mind coat the bearings and let the heat dissipate without harm to the internal parts. The extra protection they provide is necessary and well worth the additional cost. If your owner's manual or mechanic recommends one of these for your car, use it.

7

The Electrical System

Did you ever play Mr. Wizard as a kid, hold a playing card in your hand, rub your feet along the carpet, and then for the coup de grace "magically" stick the playing card on the wall—no glue, no tape, nothing up your sleeve? This may come as a surprise to you, but that little piece of legerdemain was actually a demonstration of mechanical energy being turned into electrical energy. What's more, it is the basis for many of the modern technological miracles we so often take for granted, such as the telephone and television.

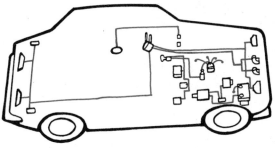

Some sort of movement is the basis for every form of energy. The source of power for each system in your car is the result of something moving in one place and that movement being transferred, usually in a different form, to someplace else. To understand this motion and to see how it is harnessed into power and how that power is transferred within your car's electrical system (the nervous system of your car), we need to look at the tiny particles that make up our world and everything in it—atoms.

Opposites Attract

Atoms (100,000,000 could fit on the head of a pin) can be broken down into three smaller parts: neutrons, protons, and electrons. All three parts have charges, either negative, positive, or neutral. These charges account for the way the particles are attracted to or repelled by each other. Neutrons have no charge, protons have a positive charge, and electrons have a negative charge. Storytellers and poets have said it for years: "opposites attract." Differences bring an element of excitement into a relationship, and while this may not always be true in our personal lives, it is true for the world of matter and energy.

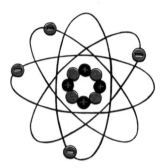

It is this world of attraction and repulsion, electromagnetism and its laws, that governs how all matter interacts. When two different materials come in contact with each other, electrons move readily from one material to the other. Objects that lose electrons become positively charged, and objects that gain electrons become negatively charged. Although electrons are always in motion, they stay attached to their original atom as long as a stronger force doesn't attract them away.

To return to the playing card experiment, remember it had no charge until we rubbed it with our hands. That rubbing brought more of the surfaces of both hands and card in contact with each other. Thus, it invited the movement of the electrons from the hands to the card, and the card received a higher negative charge. With its newfound negative charge, the playing card became attracted to the positive charge of the wall. Their opposite charges created a magnetic field that, just like any magnet, held the card to the wall until the negative charge disappeared.

This is the same magnetism that creates danger during a lightning storm: the clouds become saturated with large amounts of negative charges, the ground with positive charges. Eventually, the opposite charges are so strong that the negative charges in the clouds are irresistibly drawn to the first object they come in contact with on the positively charged ground. The full force of this monster negative electrical current and the enormous heat that is generated by that current strike the first (usually

the highest) object in the area where the positive charge is the greatest.

This is why you're told to find cover in a shelter and to avoid standing under tall trees. The tree may act as the tallest point if the positive charge is strongest there. If you're right under it, you may hear "You Light Up My Life" in stereo. It's also the reason they say if you feel your scalp or body "tingle" in the same situation, drop to your hands and knees, keeping your heart and head off the ground. The tingle you feel is the huge positive charge present in the ground. By kneeling, if there is a strike nearby, the force will hopefully be felt through your limbs, not your vital organs. Better idea still, watch the sky carefully and if there is a storm around you, get to cover. Since electricity travels at 186,000 miles per second, there may not be much in the way of a warning.

The negative particles of one matter are attracted to and move toward the positive particles of the other, so both materials get an electrical charge. Opposites attract, same charges repel; the movement is always from negative to positive. This movement, which causes the particles to move around, provides us with the stored potential energy that eventually will be converted into electrical power in the form of heat and light.

In addition to the magnetic force in which opposite charges attract and like charges repel, there is yet another magnetic force that works at right angles to the flow of current. If this magnetic force is manipulated by sending it through many tiny wires wrapped around a bar, it acts like a magnet. When set up inside a motor with a shaft, the circular pull this magnetic force generates moves the motor's shaft around and around. In this way, electrical energy becomes mechanical energy, lighting your car's lights, activating its gauges, and running many of its pumps and motors.

Measuring Electricity

The potential power of electricity is similar to water that is pumped through a pipe; if the pipe is hooked up to a wheel or turbine, the energy generated by the movement of the electrons as the water moves through the pipe can be converted into other types of energy, for example, hydroelectric power. The faster the pump turns, the faster and more intensely the water in the pipe moves and the greater the power produced. The greater the force moving the electrons, the greater the power they are capable of producing.

If the water in the pipe were to move through a smaller diameter pipe or if the pipe were rusted inside, there would be friction and more resistance to the passage of the water.

In a similar way, electrons move through wires or conductors and rub against each other as they do. The friction generated by this rubbing action not only slows down the electrons' movement it also generates heat. (Remember the friction causes heat principle from chap. 6.)

All materials offer some resistance to the movement of electrons, but some materials offer more than others. For example, silver and copper offer very little resistance and are therefore considered to be good conductors of electricity. Air, water, plastic, lead, and tin offer a lot of resistance

and therefore are considered to be poor conductors, or insulators, of electricity. Another factor that affects a conductor's resistance to the flow of electricity is its length: the longer and thinner the wire, the greater the resistance.

To know how much power is available to perform different tasks, we need to be able to measure the water in the pipe—not only how much water there is but how fast it's flowing. Similarly, we need to be able to measure the electricity in a wire—not only how many electrons are there but how fast they're moving. By counting the number of electrons that pass a given point in a wire in one second, we can measure their electrical strength or intensity. This measurement of volume is counted in amperes (amps). It is measured with an ammeter and is referred to as current. To continue the water pipe analogy, amps would be the number of gallons moving through the pipe when it's turned on. The number of amps that a bulb draws determines its brightness. For example, tail lights draw 1.5 amps; stop lights, which need to show up much brighter so you notice them when the car in front of you stops, draw 4.0 amps.

In addition, the force or pressure of electricity can be measured, not in inches or in pounds but in volts. Voltage is comparable to the pressure of the water in the pipe without being turned on; the instrument used to measure it is a voltmeter. There is one more variable whose measurement comes in handy for figuring out electrical problems. Ohms are the measurement of the resistance to the flow of electrons. An ohmmeter is the device used to measure resistance.

VOLTMETER

These three variables—the strength, the force, and the resistance to the movement of electrons through wires—are interrelated and can be mathematically calculated to determine how much electricity is moving through an object at a given point in time with respect to the demands of the object that is using the electricity. This calculation, called Ohm's law, is represented as $\frac{I=E}{M}$. It has made it possible for scientists to understand most of our world.

One other useful measurement is that of how much power is actually produced by an electrical current. Instead of choosing an arbitrary chore like a weight being lifted off the ground for a certain period of time, which we call horsepower, electricity is measured in watts, and for convenience, since it takes a bunch of watts to do almost anything, it is measured in thousands or kilowatts and kilowatt-hours. Kilowatts keep us from stumbling over our zeros. An electrical load, the measurement for power consumed by a motor or light, is measured in watts. The higher the wattage, the brighter the bulb.

=HORSEPOWER

=WATTS

Think of these variables and the laws that govern them as tools in an electrical toolbox. You may not actually use them, but it helps to understand what they are and do in order to understand your car's electrical system.

Circuits

If you were to take apart the inside of an ordinary lamp, you would see two wires, one leading into the base of the lamp and one leading away from it. Electricity that is generated by huge power stations, sometimes many miles away, comes into our homes, in the form of current through different circuits (groups of lights or accessories that are connected electrically) and gives us heat and light and then returns to its source, the power station. For electricity to flow, it must be able to return to its source; without a return loop, a complete pathway, it's not going anywhere.

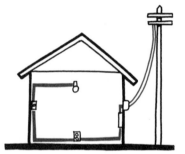

In your car as well as in your home, electricity needs to return to its source and is divided into circuits. Today's cars have four circuits, starting, charging, ignition, and accessories. More about them later. In your home, a return wire completes the circuit, but in cars, it is the frame of the car that completes the circuit. The use of the car's metal frame as the return loop is referred to as grounding. An understanding of proper grounding is the key to understanding how your car's electrical system works and why it sometimes doesn't.

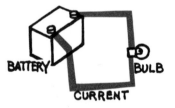

BATTERY   BULB

CURRENT

Current travels through a series of wires joined by connectors (sometimes wire to wire, sometimes one wire will branch at a connector into 3 or 4 wires) to the accessory or light and returns to the battery, not through another skinny little wire but through the frame of the car. Since

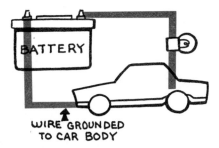

WIRE GROUNDED
TO CAR BODY

the material the frame is made of is a good conductor of electrical current, it is used as the return wire for all circuits. This saves on the amount of wiring, which particularly in today's electricity-hungry cars already looks like a spaghetti factory gone berserk.

Switches and Relays

Each circuit has a switch that acts as a gate and serves as a bridge or a conductor for the electrical current, turning the current off and on. A switch is a piece of metal suspended between two pieces of wire. When the switch touches both wires, it closes a "gate." For example, when you turn on the headlights for night driving, a switch shuts the gate for that lighting circuit, the circuit is complete, and current flows to the headlights. The lights are illuminated by the heat and light generated by that electrical current. If the switch does not touch both wires, the circuit is open. In other words, there is a gap of air between the wires that carry the current. Air is an insulator, not a conductor of current; it prevents the passage of electricity. Consequently, the flow of current is interrupted and the gate is open. Theoretically, switches only open or close gates, allowing the current to flow by completing the circuit, when they're told to do so.

So that you don't have to stop and plug each individual wire into each circuit when you want to use different accessories, you simply hit a switch for the accessory that you want to work, the gate closes, the circuit is complete, and the current flows. Switches on your car are either manually operated like the headlights, where you pull or push a knob or lever, or mechanically operated like the brakes.

Relays, like runners in a relay race, pass on something,

CONNECTORS

SWITCH

RELAY

HOUSE ROCKER TOGGLE DASH

DOOR SWITCH

7.15

in this case, current. These backup safety switches are used on circuits in which the current that develops is so strong a regular switch can't handle it, for example, the ignition, the windshield wiper motor, and the horn. They use a small amount of current to control a large amount of current.

Just as any metal or plastic device can malfunction, so can switches and relays. A relay can simply stop working, and current will not flow to the accessory in its charge. A switch can become stuck in the ON position, completing the circuit so there is current going to the light or accessory constantly—even when you assume it's not. Even if the accessory or light doesn't use a lot of amps, it doesn't take long before the reserve current of the battery is completely used up, and you have a dead battery and a dead car on your hands. Recharging the battery and replacing the switch will usually solve the problem.

Fuses

Fuses and fusible links, like circuit breakers, guard the electrical system from fires resulting from overheating as a consequence of too much electricity. These surges of excess electricity can result from having too many accessories on one circuit or from the insulation being torn or frayed.

Most accessories, except for the headlights, have fuses that are wires contained within plastic or glass tubes. If too much voltage surges through a circuit and causes it to get too hot, the wire element in the fuse melts or "blows." Consequently, there is a gap of air that causes the gate to open and stops the flow of current. The circuit has been broken.

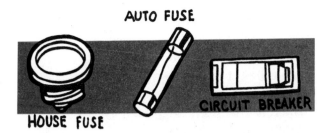

AUTO FUSE

HOUSE FUSE

CIRCUIT BREAKER

If you don't know where the fuse box is located in your car, look in your owner's manual or have your mechanic show you. And while you're at it, find out what a burned-out fuse looks like and the easiest way to replace one. Be sure you carry extra fuses that are the correct size as indicated in your owner's manual. If there is a problem anywhere in your car's electrical system, check first to see whether there is a fuse for that accessory. If there is, examine it to see whether it is blown before you send for help. It is an all too common occurrence today for cars to be towed into dealerships and service stations when the problem could have been remedied with an inexpensive fuse. Don't waste your time and money.

Fusible links accomplish the same thing as fuses, but rather than being enclosed in glass or plastic and placed together in a box, they are thinner pieces of wire located at strategic points in the wiring. If there is a surge of current, the thinner wire melts and the circuit is broken. Circuit breakers are spring loaded devices that retract when they receive a current surge. To be without the use of an accessory because a fuse, fusible link, or circuit breaker has melted or sprung may be very inconvenient temporarily but well worth it to avoid a greater inconvenience—a fire.

Solving Electrical Problems

Electrical problems inevitably result from the inability of voltage to get from the power supply to the component and back again. This inability to deliver the current successfully and return home is usually the result of a "short" or an "open."

Logically and by definition, a short is a circuit that is accidentally shortened; the current doesn't reach its destination, whether that is a light or an accessory. A short may be the result of the insulating material around the wire wearing away either by contact with another piece of metal or general wear and tear. Stripped of its insulation, the wire can touch against the metal of the car body. The wire's current will return to the battery never having reached the accessory or light for which it was intended. It will have completed the circuit but not have delivered the current. Current doesn't know where it's supposed to go, and it won't know that it never reached the light or accessory; it only knows it should always take the quickest and easiest path home, and that, through the frame, is just what it did.

If a fuse is replaced and it blows again immediately, it could be that there is a wire having intermittent contact with the metal frame caused by the vibration of the car as it travels along the road. If it happens often and can't be traced, the only answer is to replace the wiring in that circuit.

Things would be a lot simpler if a short always caused a fuse to blow—you would know immediately there was a problem in that particular circuit—but it doesn't. Furthermore, an open will also cause current to be interrupted. If a wire were actually broken or frayed in such a way that air was between the two pieces of wire, it would act as an insulator, not a conductor, and interrupt the flow of current. The air would act as a switch acts when it's not on. An open may be in the form of a broken wire, a bad switch, a burned-out bulb, a malfunctioning motor, or a faulty connection. If a connector is dirty or corroded, resistance is raised in that circuit. Cleaning or replacing the connector should correct the problem.

Electrical problems are sneak thieves that rob your battery of its stored electricity and turn mechanics into bloodhounds. They must follow the path of the electrical circuit to discover where the culprits, shorts and opens, are hiding. For each car, there is a color-coded diagram available which shows all its circuits. Like any road map, some diagrams are easier to read than others. Checking any circuit is a logical, not difficult, testing process that any competent mechanic with sufficient patience and the proper tools can do.

To discover a current drain, a mechanic uses a test

lamp. To find out which circuit the drain is in, each fuse is removed and replaced one at a time until the test light goes out, indicating that is the circuit where the drain is hiding. The mechanic's next step is to reconnect the battery and see if that circuit's accessory or light is on all the time. If it is, the culprit has been found, and the faulty switch, which kept the gate closed and electricity flowing all the time, is usually replaced.

If the culprit is not a switch, an ohmmeter can be used to continue the hunt. The wiring and all connectors need to be checked all the way back to the battery. If the needle on the ohmmeter moves, it means current is passing through the circuit at that point. If the needle doesn't move, current is not passing at that point. It is up to the tracker to backtrack along the wire to find where the current stopped.

If faulty wiring is not at fault and there is still power at the closest connector to a light or accessory, the ground (the place where it is attached to the frame of the car) of either the light or accessory should be checked. Very often the ground for a light or motor is the bolt or mount that attaches the light or accessory to the car. If this attachment is dirty, rusted, corroded, loose, or missing, the ground will be inadequate and there won't be a complete circuit. If the ground looks good, there is still one more test before an accessory or motor should be replaced—hooking it up to a known good ground. A section of wire could have been overlooked by the tracker.

If the ground is bad for one accessory, it may seek a ground through another that's off. If it does, it can cause the other seemingly unrelated accessory to turn on. Some of the most bizarre electrical activity results from the fact that there is often more than one circuit on a ground. For example, you push in the lighter and the dashboard glows! Finding the bad ground and repairing it should correct this strange behavior.

Starting, Charging, and Ignition Circuits

We'll show here what each circuit includes so that if you ever have a problem you'll be able to identify the pieces. The starting circuit consists of battery ignition switch, starter, starter switch, wires, and frame. The charging circuit consists of battery, alternator (generator), voltage regulator, wires, and frame. A traditional ignition circuit consists of battery, ignition, switch, coil, distributor, spark plugs; an electronic ignition adds the electronic control module (computer).

As with all the systems in this book, however, it is important to remember that we are not listing every item of every system. Since we've already discussed the starting, charging, and ignition systems in chapters 3 and 4, most of the rest of this chapter will concentrate on accessories.

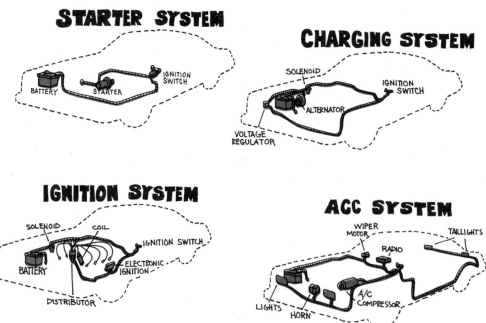

Lights

The light system includes brake lights, headlights, side-markers, directional lights, license plate lights, and hazard lights, which are all mandatory on today's cars. Most lights operate in a similar manner: wires run through and into a bulb that is attached to a tungsten filament, a piece

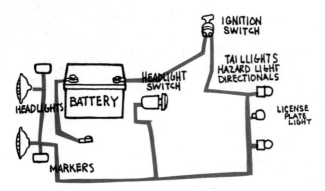

of fine wire. Current flows to the bulb through the wire and the socket and then on to the filament. The current causes tiny particles in the filament to heat up. The tiny particles heat up so much they literally fly through the air and send out showers of glowing sparks. This glow is called incandescence. Eventually, the filament wears out, and the bulb burns out. Bulbs would burn out very quickly if they were not sealed and filled with argon, a gas that prevents oxygen from entering and causing the filament to burn away immediately. A bulb can contain more than one filament in it, as do, for example, tail lights and stoplights and some headlights.

Headlights age over time in addition to burning out completely. They will begin to show a darkening, which means that the metal of the filament is burning off and collecting on the inside of the bulb. If this happens, have the headlight changed, or if you know that your car's headlights are simple to change, you may want to do it yourself. Don't assume simplicity, however; some headlights require special tools and much work—even removing the entire grille! Aging headlights prevent you from seeing the road properly at night.

Get in the habit of checking all lights once a month. You won't always notice the absence of one out of four headlights. Ask someone to sit in the car and help determine the health of your backup, tail, and brake lights as well. The car will need to be running to check directionals and backup lights. Avoid endangering yourself or being stopped by the police.

If there's one dim headlight, a corroded terminal or a faulty seal could be the culprit. For headlight dimming or malfunctioning in conjunction with starting problems, check the condition of the battery first.

If the directional lights don't work, both the front and rear bulbs should be checked. Replacing the burned out bulb should put the system right again. The replacement of bulbs on newer cars is often made easier with removable plastic panels for easy access instead of having to take apart the entire lens. Check your owner's manual to see if there are any diagrams to show you the easy way to change the bulbs in your car.

If you have a light that works intermittently, suspect the bulb's socket; it may be dirty, corroded, or loose. An interior light may stay on because of a stuck switch. If more than one bulb is out or a bulb and another accessory are both out, suspect the wiring for the circuit. If the same bulb burns out often, the cause could be too much current. A faulty alternator or regulator, often caused by a bad ground, could be responsible.

The flasher unit is a switch that turns the directional bulbs on and off 60 to 120 times per minute; it also activates the flashing emergency hazard lights.

Dashboard Instrumentation

The instrumentation circuit is made up of gauges and warning lights. All the dashboard lights should go on

when you turn the car on and then go out immediately after. If a warning light doesn't work when the car is turned on, it could be the bulb. If all the dashboard lights are out, the culprit is more likely a fuse, a damaged wire, or a faulty dash ground. A flickering dash light may be caused by a loose or corroded ground.

If a gauge doesn't work when the car is turned on, the fuse should be checked first, then the sending unit (a sensor that relays volume and temperature information to the gauge), and last the gauge. If all gauges are reading erratically, however, the wiring and connectors, fuse dash ground, and the alternator and voltage regulator should be checked.

Windshield Wiper

The windshield wiper system is run by a small electrical motor that creates rotational motion (there is usually only one for both wipers). The motor has a connecting arm that transfers its rotational motion to the side-to-side motion of the wiper arms.

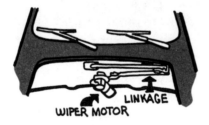

LINKAGE
WIPER MOTOR

Wiper motors have a fuse and at least one or possibly two switches. The second switch allows the wiper arm to continue moving until it returns to its original position after you shut it off. In winter, windshield wipers often get overloaded from too much snow or the arm freezes to the windshield. If they stop working, it could be just a blown fuse, not a failed motor. If the fuse is okay, the switch and the ground should be checked before the motor is replaced. If one wiper works but the other doesn't, the motor is probably not the problem. The linkage between the two wiper arms should be examined to see it is still securely connected. If the wipers work at one speed but not at another, have the switch and wiring checked.

A reservoir stores a special cleaning fluid containing additives to keep it from freezing in winter. Check this reservoir periodically and replenish it with additional fluid as needed. Of all the fluids in your car, it may seem the least important, but it won't be if you're driving on a wet highway and an 18-wheeler passes you, lathering your windshield with mud from all of its 18 wheels. Your safety depends on good visibility—don't take a chance on going for the wiper fluid when you need it and discovering that it's dry as a bone. Murphy's law says the road won't be.

Keep windshield and wiper blades clean with cleaning solvent, and replace the blades as they wear. Often their wear will show up as an irregular or streaky wiper pattern—guaranteed to develop directly in your line of vision if you are the driver. Be sure, however, that this is not the result of a bent blade. If you live in an area where there are severe ice and snow accumulations, switch to winter blades. These heavier, softer rubber blades cost more but will handle ice and snow far better than conventional blades. One good ice storm will convince you of their worth. Have your mechanic change them or buy them from an auto parts store. If you're a Do-It-Yourselfer, be sure the parts people show you exactly how to remove the old blades and install the new ones. For reasons I cannot understand, there are certain blades whose attachments defy both logic and normal intelligence. If your blades look as though you need to be a rocket scientist to install them, have your mechanic replace them for you and pay the extra charge for labor willingly. It will be worth the additional charge for the absence of the aggravation.

The Horn

A car starts backing out from the parking spot ahead of you, and you know the van parked next to it is blocking the driver's vision. It's collision course ahead. You push on the steering wheel and give a blast of the horn to alert the other car to the danger. Nothing. What really happened?

The button that lies beneath the leather or plastic of the steering wheel sent an electrical current to a magnet, which pulled a plunger attached to a thin disc, called a diaphragm, the vibrations of which should have converted the

CAR HORN

DOOR BELL

silent electric impulses to an audible signal. As the diaphragm moved inward, it caused a set of metal arms (contact points) to separate, resulting in the loss of magnetic force. Without the pull of the magnet, the plunger and diaphragm released. The process happens over and over again. Moving the diaphragm back and forth rapidly generates a vibration that emits a noise, whose signal is directed through the cone of the horn where it is amplified.

The main problem areas for the horn are three: the button can't make the contact (usually because it has become bent), the relay fails, or the ground is bad or missing. To be sure the horn on your car is working correctly, give it a blast on a regular basis. The thing about horns, especially in today's crowded parking lots, is that when you need them you really need them.

Solving Electrical Problems

What is important to remember about automotive circuits is that often there are unrelated accessories on one circuit. Different accessories will have the same wiring and the same fuse. If there's a problem, a mechanic would have a hard time finding it without a diagram.

If the electrical problem your car is experiencing is weird—electrical problems are notorious for that—your regular mechanic may not be able to help. If that's the case, as usual, get on the phone and do some homework. Start by asking your mechanic who does the shop's electric work.

Although many specialty shops advertise "electrical"

work, they often aren't equipped to do any more than simple parts replacement, for example, alternators and voltage regulators. If the shop doesn't have good wiring diagrams, and there's a particularly difficult problem they're dealing with, you'll often wind up paying extra for the time it takes them to diagnose (if they are able) the problem correctly. So check around before you put yourself and your wiring in the hands of strangers.

CAUTION: If while driving you detect the odor of burning rubber or plastic, it could be the wiring insulation burning away from or rubbing against the metal of the body. This is a warning to be heeded. Have the electrical system checked out as soon as possible. A short circuit may be about to eliminate the functioning of one of your handy accessories or lights, or worse yet, it could be the start of an electrical fire

If it is a fire, drive the car to a safe area, stop, pull the inside hood latch, and get yourself and your passengers out of the car and to safety immediately. Go to the nearest phone and call the fire department. Do *not* open the hood of the car. The extra oxygen that is added by opening the hood may fan the fire more. You have already helped by releasing the hood's interior latch. Stay away from the car while you are awaiting the arrival of the fire department and let professionals put the fire out.

8

The Power Train

Transmissions: The Link of Power

Did you ever push a car? You start out feeling as though it is cemented to the ground. You're pretty sure this is a lesson in how to get a hernia. The car—all 2,500-plus pounds of it—sits there while you grunt, groan, grumble, push, heave, and sweat. But then as you continue to push, it starts to move. Gradually, it begins to move easier, and soon it's rolling along almost effortlessly. You, the pusher, are feeling less like Pee Wee and more like Arnold Swarzenegger every minute. Why, this car-pushing business doesn't seem so bad after all!

But wait, here's a little upward slope. The car seems to be gaining weight again, and you're back to grunting and

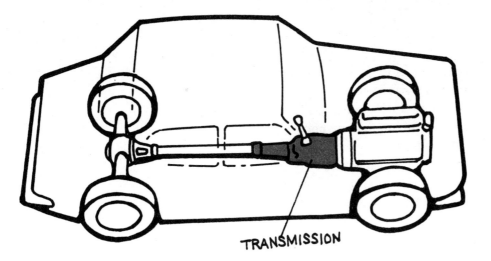

TRANSMISSION

groaning. You struggle, exhausted, to the top of the incline.
But before you have time to pat yourself on the back for a
job well done, the car crests the hill and begins rolling
down the slope on the other side. Oh, no. All of a sudden
you can barely hold the darn car back, and now you're
doing your impression of Edwin Moses trying to catch up
with it before it runs over that shiny little sports car with
its horrified driver sitting right in your path.

One of Isaac Newton's (the fellow with the apple in the
tower) laws of motion has just been demonstrated. Things
in motion want to stay in motion, unless disturbed by an

outside force. Things at rest want to stay at rest. Inertia (a
phenomenon my father swore my five brothers and I rede-
fined as we sat glued to the TV while he juggled three full
bags of groceries and the front door knob at the same time)
places resistance on the car's forward motion from a dead
stop. However, once the car is moving, it wants to keep
moving. (Dad never could understand how we could have
missed the second part of this law, when we had mastered
the first part so well.) The car's heavy weight, which had
made it so difficult to move initially, is now the factor that

keeps it moving. Having broken with the force of inertia, the only forms of resistance to its forward motion are the air, a physical barrier (e.g., large walls, sports cars), or a greater force trying to change its direction (e.g., you trying to stop it). Momentum, the force of motion, has taken over.

To compensate for these natural forces, cars need slow powerful turns from their wheels to get going from a stop, when traveling up hills, or when carrying a heavy load. But they need speedy turns from their wheels when they're going down the road at highway speeds. It is the job of the transmission to meet those different needs, for it is the "link" between the engine and the wheels.

Let's go back to the bicycle analogy in chapter 1. Remember it was through the bicycle chain that the energy produced by the pumping action of the bicyclist's legs was passed along to the bicycle wheels? Attached to that chain were gears, those metal toothed wheels that produced the different wheel power necessary for going up hills and down. Just as the 10-speed gears transmit different power to the bicycle wheels for different conditions, so do the gears of the transmission. To meet the changing needs of the car, the energy produced by the pumping action of the pistons has to be transmitted differently to the car's wheels—sometimes powerfully, sometimes speedily, sometimes not at all.

There are two types of transmissions to choose from: standard (manual) and automatic. Since a standard transmission is simpler, let's look at it first.

Manual Transmissions

With a manual or standard transmission, you are the chief. You select the gear appropriate for the changing needs of the car by moving a stick called a gear shift lever, which on newer cars is usually located on the floor. But what happens if you choose the wrong gear, if you daydream at a stoplight and forget that the car is in fourth gear? The car stalls, Godzilla in the car behind you beeps his horn impatiently, and you get to restart the car, don't you? Fourth gear doesn't have the power required to overcome the force of inertia and move the car from a stop. It is a speedy gear to be used only when the car is moving at a

fairly rapid pace. Had you chosen first gear, a slow powerful gear, the car would have started forward like a champ. Driving a standard transmission means you're responsible for selecting the correct gear. If you choose incorrectly, you and your car deal with the consequences.

How Gears Work

Gears work on the principle that the faster the engine turns in relation to the wheels, the more power (torque) is produced. Remember—from a start or going up a hill, your car needs big, slow, powerful turns from its wheels, but once it's rolling, it wants many speedy turns.

Within most transmissions are found two sets of gears, side by side. On one end, they are attached to the engine by a round metal bar called the input shaft; on the other end, they are attached to the wheels by the output shaft. To see how gears really work, let's start with first gear. The big gear, attached to the wheels, has 40 teeth; the small gear, attached to the engine, has 10. If these two gears mesh or lock together, how many times will the small gear go around in the time it takes the large gear to go around once? The answer "four" would have rocketed you to the head of the class. The turning force (torque) of four speedy turns of the input shaft are transferred into one slow powerful turn of the output shaft. This relationship is expressed as a gear ratio. The gear ratio for this set of gears is 4:1. This first or low gear works well for a car that is starting out from a dead stop when the wheels need to turn powerfully, not speedily.

As the car continues to move forward, having broken with the force of inertia, it needs less power and more speed. In first gear, four speedy turns of the input shaft were transferred into one powerful turn of the output shaft. In second gear, the gear attached to the wheels may have 30 teeth and the gear attached to the engine may have 10 teeth. Three speedy turns of the input shaft are transferred into one slower turn of the output shaft (gear ratio 3:1). Second gear is still a powerful gear but not as powerful as first. As the car continues to approach highway speeds, the slow powerful turns of the wheels are no longer needed. Instead, speedy input shaft turns are required to transfer directly into speedy output shaft

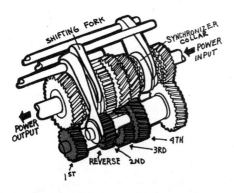

turns. Eventually, when the car reaches highway speeds, the force of inertia has been broken, and the force of momentum has taken over. The gear attached to the engine and the gear attached to the wheel have the same number of teeth. Consequently, in high gear (third or fourth depending on the gear box), both gears are turning at the same speed (gear ratio 3:3). High gear transfers lots of speed but little power. Gear reduction demonstrates the principle that power increases as speed decreases.

This progression of less power/more speed goes on until the car is cruising at highway speeds and on a flat road. Here, a fifth gear can take even greater advantage of the car's momentum. With mostly speed rather than power a requirement for this type of driving, the gear attached to the engine can turn less than the gear attached to the wheel (gear ratio 0.85:l). Fewer turns of the input shaft mean the engine doesn't work as much; therefore, it doesn't use as much gas. Consequently, you save money by using fifth gear on flat roads at highway speeds.

But wait. Here comes that hill again. The car begins to climb. The car needs power once again. You'll need to drop down to a more powerful gear such as fourth or third, or even second, in order to get the power that the car requires. When buying a car, assess how much driving you will do at highway speeds before paying the additional money for fifth gear. If you do mostly stop-and-go driving, the extra expense may not be worth it.

Reverse gear does just as you might have expected; it reverses the forward motion of the wheels. Because, ideally, the car is stopped before you reverse its direction, it will need a very powerful slow gear to get it going, so reverse gear is tied to first gear.

With all this meshing and unmeshing of different

gears, you might think they'd wear like other moving engine parts. Well, at one time, they did. The earliest gears actually moved into and out of each other, sometimes meshing smoothly, sometimes not. When two gears meshed together their separate rotations had to be coordinated or—*crunch, crunch*—the gear teeth bumped into each other. The result was missing teeth and general gear wear. Then came synchronizers.

In today's gear boxes, it is the synchronizers—bronze rings with teeth (dogs) that point out and collars with teeth that point in—that actually move, not the gears. The gear ratios are already locked together. The synchronizers slow down in order to equalize the speed of the rotations. Only when the parts are rotating at the same speed are the new gear combinations locked into place and called into active duty. This makes for smooth shifting, few crunches, and very little wear on the gears themselves. So, gears rarely wear out (unless they are driven particularly long and hard); the synchronizers do instead. Such a deal.

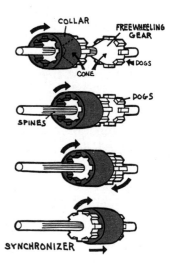

The Clutch

What's the purpose of a clutch? Do you remember that we talked about minimum engine revolutions per minute (rpms) in chapter 4? And how if the crankshaft doesn't turn at least 750 rpms, it will stall? Well, there's just one small detail about a crankshaft that turns at 750 rpms: 750 rpms equals 15 miles per hour (mph). Nothing wrong with that, you say. That's true, until you coast up to a stoplight. There he is, your friendly police officer directing traffic. To avoid stalling, you (a) carefully run the stoplight

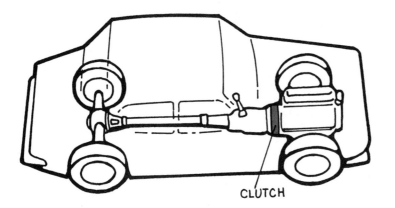

at 15 mph, hoping the officer will understand; (b) turn the car off for this and every other stoplight, stop sign, jaywalker, and so on, or (c) use the clutch and stop for the light.

It is the clutch that permits the engine, which must maintain a minimum speed to avoid stalling, to continue to run without transmitting that speed to the wheels. While it's called the "connector," it is also the "disconnector." The clutch temporarily disconnects the wheels from the engine so that the engine can run, but the wheels don't know about it. Keeping this little secret from the wheels means that you can move from one gear to another. It also means you don't have to turn the car off at every light or make a hobby of collecting traffic tickets.

How does a clutch work? There are two basic types of clutches—spring and diaphragm. Spring clutches are more expensive and are disappearing from use, so we'll concentrate on the diaphragm clutch.

A diaphragm clutch assembly consists of the flywheel, three steel plates or discs that slide along a shaft, a round metal doughnut called a throw-out bearing, and a metal arm called a release fork. A clutch cover keeps dirt and foreign matter out of the system. We'll begin with the plates.

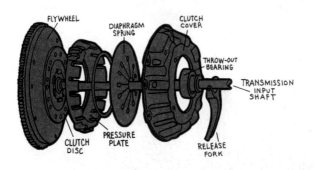

Since you already know from chapter 4 what the flywheel looks like, we'll skip that and go to the clutch disc. It has a row of small metal teeth on its inner circumference which allow it to slide back and forth on a shaft that has metal teeth on its outside circumference. These teeth are called splines, and the bar they move back and forth on is a splined shaft—the transmission input shaft. The next plate in line is the pressure plate. This plate has a large hole cut out of its center and is bolted to the flywheel. The third plate, called a diaphragm spring, is shaped like a cone and made out of flexible steel. The throw-out bearing and release fork secure the diaphragm spring and other components to the shaft.

The clutch disc is covered with a tough friction material called a lining. Think of this material as a sneaker. That's right. A sneaker. If you put a sneaker on and scuff your foot along the kitchen floor, friction results and your foot sticks to the floor, doesn't it? Likewise for the clutch disc. Because it is lined with sneakerlike material, when the disc scuffs against another surface, it also sticks. To really understand how this clutch works, try the following exercise.

Look at your two palms. Pretend one palm is the clutch disc and the other is the flywheel. Press your two palms together hard. Now try rotating one without letting up on the pressure. Difficult to do, isn't it? They both turn as one. Now press your palms together with very little pressure. Now try rotating one. One hand slips and slides rather easily, not turning with the other one, doesn't it? The clutch works on a similar principle.

A series of metal rods connects the clutch components to the clutch pedal, which is found to the left of the brake pedal. To engage the clutch, you release the clutch pedal

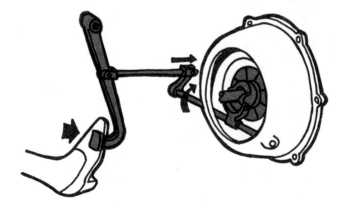

completely. This causes the the diaphragm spring to take back its conical shape. In its natural state the rim of the diaphragm puts pressure on the pressure plate which forces the discs forward against the flywheel. The clutch disc's sneakerlike lining generates friction as it comes in contact with the whizzing flywheel. Just as the two palms when pressed together with great force turned as one, so now does the clutch disc and the flywheel. The clutch components begin to turn at the same rate that the crankshaft is turning. Depending on the gear selected, the clutch disc will go from rest (0 rpm) to as few as 750 rpms and as many as 5,000 rpms or more! If the engine is running and the clutch pedal is released, the flywheel and clutch components, including the clutch disc, are turning as one. Because the clutch disc is attached to the transmission by the splined shaft it moves back and forth on, power is now flowing to the transmission and to the wheels. The wheels now know that the engine is turning so they begin to move.

When you push the clutch pedal all the way in (down) to disengage the clutch, the release fork pushes the throw-out bearing forward, resulting in pressure on the center of the diaphragm spring. As the center of the spring moves inward, its rim moves outward; the pressure that was pushing the pressure plate and disc against the flywheel is eliminated. Consequently, the clutch disc, which had been squeezed against the flywheel, separates from it and sits idle—disconnected now from the engine's turning crankshaft. The link of power has been broken and will not return until the clutch is again engaged by returning the clutch pedal to its up position. With no power being passed to the wheels, the transmission is now in a neutral state. The wheels are oblivious to the fact that the engine is still running—producing enough power to keep from stalling but not transferring that power to them. It's a good thing, too: here comes another stoplight and another police officer.

Checking Manual Transmission Fluid
There are some things about the clutch that it pays to know if you want yours to be around for a while. Be sure to have the manual transmission fluid checked by a professional every six months or whenever your owner's manual says. While there is a dipstick under the hood on a few cars, manual transmission fluid is usually checked by removing a filler plug located under the car. This is a job best done by a professional while the car is on a lift. Man-

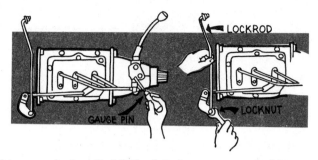

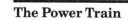
ual transmission fluid (the kind recommended in your manual) should be added if necessary.

A manual transmission doesn't get as hot as an automatic transmission does, so it can go a fairly long time between checks. But you never know when a transmission seal will break and the fluid leak out. Without the correct amount of this dark and stinky fluid, the now-familiar metal, metal, friction, heat, wear routine will inevitably occur. A warning sign that the fluid may be low is stiffness, difficulty, or strange grinding noises when shifting gears. Never let repair work be done on your transmission until the transmission fluid level has been checked. It's such a simple service that I have it done whenever my car is on a lift, whether for changing the oil or putting on snow tires.

Important Facts about Clutch Wear
As you release the clutch pedal, the clutch disc has to hustle to catch up and connect with the spinning flywheel. This "catch-up" phase that occurs before the connection is complete corresponds to pressing your palms together with little pressure. Remember the slipping motion that resulted? In the fraction of a second that it takes the disc to catch up to the flywheel, the disc slips and slides. This slipping motion produces friction that results in extremely high temperatures and causes wear.

Fortunately, the disc lining is designed to withstand high temperatures but only for a short time. The key word here is "short." The clutch needs to connect and disconnect quickly. If you rest your foot on the clutch pedal all the time, you "ride the clutch." Even though you may not feel it, the pressure of your foot may be just enough for the throw-out bearing to begin turning and for the clutch disc to go into its catch-up phase.

You get a little help in avoiding premature clutch wear from the design of the clutch pedal: for the first inch or so that you push the pedal in, you won't feel any resistance. This "free play" helps to keep you from activating the disc inadvertently. The problem is, even though you may not feel resistance, the clutch components may be turning. The only real safeguard to premature clutch wear is to keep your foot off the clutch pedal when not in use; engage it, change gears, and then get off it altogether, even if you don't have anything else special to do with that foot. If you are stuck at a light on a hill with no way to break the boredom except to move the car back and forth by playing with the clutch pedal, try to restrain yourself. It will cost you money in premature clutch service if you don't. Use the parking brake to hold the car steady on hills if necessary.

FREE PLAY

Besides wearing away clutch components at a rapid rate, riding the clutch also contributes to glazing: the disc lining forms a glaze, a thin layer of ice that never melts. Previously in this chapter I talked about the clutch disc lining acting as a sneaker would, causing your foot to stick when you scuffed it along the kitchen floor. If you were to put a glass slipper on that same foot (What! Do you mean you've never worn one?) and scuff it along the same floor, your foot would slip and slide, wouldn't it? That's what happens to a clutch disc once a glaze has formed on it. Instead of sticking like a sneaker when it comes in contact with the flywheel, it slips like a glass slipper. The connection is no longer sure, and the wheels struggle to catch up with the engine. We'll see in chapter 11 that this is also true for brake pads, which are made out of similar material and which respond in a similar way to high heat.

Riding the clutch is just a habit. If you have it, break it. This may take some concentrated effort. But even if you're careful and you don't ride the clutch, eventually the disc lining and other components wear out. As the lining wears, it becomes thinner, causing the disc to travel farther to connect with the flywheel. When this happens, the pedal will begin to grab higher and higher before it connects. You will no longer feel a crisp, sure connection as the clutch pedal rises off the floor and the engine and wheels finally connect.

If, as you lift your foot off the clutch pedal, there is a

long hesitation and the clutch pedal is almost at the top of its rise before it grabs, if the car shakes, shudders, or bucks before it moves forward, or the engine races, but the car doesn't seem to go as fast as the sound of the turning engine suggests, or if it takes more rpms than it previously did to travel uphill, the clutch assembly may simply need an adjustment.

Adjusting the Clutch

Some cars adjust automatically; some do not. You will need to check your owner's manual to see if a clutch adjustment is recommended for your car. Somehow compensation has to be made for the lining's decreasing thickness as well as the stretching of the rods and levers, known as "linkage," that connect the clutch to the clutch pedal and transmission. Most manual transmissions have either a hydraulic (fluid under pressure) or mechanical (cable) clutch, which should be adjusted by a professional every 25,000 to 30,000 miles or whenever your owner's manual recommends. If yours is hydraulic, be sure to have the clutch fluid checked while you're at it.

If you experience any of the above symptoms and an adjustment is recommended for your car, don't wait. Make arrangements to have that service done as soon as possible. A simple adjustment now will reduce clutch wear and save you early and expensive replacement costs. Clutch work is expensive—the last thing you need is for it to be premature.

Eventually, if the lining is not replaced, the clutch disc loses all of its friction-generating capability; if not replaced, it simply "burns out." No connection is made and the wheels refuse to turn as the engine races merrily on. Regardless of the condition of your sinuses, long before this

final stage occurred you would have been notified by a pungent burning odor.

If the clutch disc needs replacement (usually with normal use, after 70,000 miles), it's a good idea to have the mechanic look carefully at all the interior components including the pressure plate and flywheel. If the clutch disc's lining was too worn the metal disc may have scratched the surface of the flywheel. The flywheel may have to be resurfaced by putting it on a special machine that removes the top layer of metal, thus making it smooth again. This procedure drives the ante up. Better to do it while the clutch is apart rather than in three months. The tough and expensive part about clutch work is the labor involved in dismantling it and putting it back together again.

To avoid major repairs, have the clutch service done when it is recommended in your manual and pay attention when your car asks for more power. It will share with you a variety of sounds if you leave it in a speedy gear when it's asking for a powerful gear—like when you're traveling uphill with the entire Girl Scout troop seated in the back seat. Eventually, it will vibrate, shudder, and buck. Don't be afraid to downshift. This is not a recommendation to wind the transmission out in second gear so that the poor thing screams in pain for want of a higher gear. Be kind. Be considerate. Your car will likely return your kindness many times over. But even if it doesn't, don't panic. Read on for ways to minimize repair expenses if it does fail you.

Automatic Transmissions

With an automatic transmission, you hire a mechanical device, similar to a brain, to decide which gear is correct

for different driving conditions. This hydraulic device, by definition, uses fluid under pressure, specifically, transmission fluid, to select the correct gear and to do the shifting for you.

Along with its brain (the valve control body) and about a zillion other parts, including gears, a pump, bands, and clutches, an automatic transmission has a "torque converter" that connects and disconnects the power of the engine from the wheels so that you don't have to. A torque converter is the automatic transmissions version of a clutch.

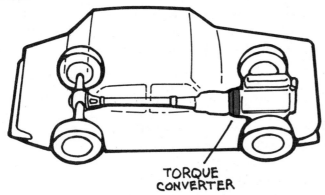

TORQUE
CONVERTER

Inside the torque converter there are two bowls placed opposite each other. Inside each is a fan, the kind you use to keep yourself cool in the summer. One fan is called an impeller and is bolted to the flywheel. The other fan is called a turbine and is attached to the transmission input shaft. Within these bowls there is a lightweight oil called transmission fluid. A transmission pump pressurizes the fluid.

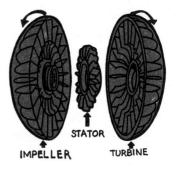

STATOR

IMPELLER   TURBINE

As the car's engine runs, the flywheel turns, causing the impeller to turn. If the flywheel is turning fast enough, this causes the transmission fluid to swirl and spill over into the turbine. A vaned wheel called a stator causes the fluid to turn in one direction only. When the engine is at very low speed, the fluid may not turn forcefully enough to move the turbine at all, and no motion will be passed to the turbine and therefore none to the wheels. Only when the engine picks up speed does the fluid circulate with enough force to turn the turbine, the output shaft, and therefore the wheels. Obviously, the more speed the engine develops, the faster the turbine spins.

Meanwhile, down below in Command Central (the valve control body), the turbine's motion affects the pressure of the fluid within the many tiny passageways. Each passageway has its own valve that regulates the flow of fluid, allowing it to empty or fill. The valves receive signals indicating vehicle speed and throttle pressure which cause the different valves to open or close and passageways to empty or fill with fluid. Each passageway is connected to a servo, a pistonlike device. When the passageway fills, the servos are activated. They then push against other parts of the transmission, the bands and clutches that are ultimately responsible for which gear is selected.

As the engine picks up speed, in response to increased pressure on the accelerator, the turbine turns faster, pressure in the valve control body rises, another passageway is filled, and another servo is activated, which selects a higher, speedier, gear. And all the driver has to do is select a position on the selecto-lever and step on the gas.

Planetary Gears
The gears within an automatic transmission may not look like the ones within a manual transmission, but the principle of gear reduction is the same: sets of gears (two, three, or four depending on the gearbox, plus Reverse) multiply the speedy turning force of smaller gears into the powerful turning force of larger gears.

The difference is in how the gears multiply that force. In a manual transmission, the gear sets responsible for gear reductions sit side by side. In an automatic transmission, the gear sets take the form of planetary gears. Each planetary gear set consists of an outer ring gear within which sits a central (sun) gear flanked by smaller planet

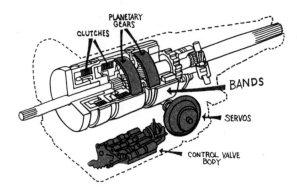

gears. These smaller planet gears move around the central gear and are connected by a planet carrier.

Different gear ratios are selected, not by movement back and forth to engage different gear sets, as in a manual transmission, but by locking one piece of the gear set while allowing another to turn. It is the servos that put pressure on tiny packs of clutches (miniature versions of the ones we looked at earlier in this chapter) and bands (round metal collars) that lock and release specific parts of the gear sets, either sun gears, ring gears, or planet carriers. As portions of the gear sets are locked into action, they automatically transfer whatever speed or power they have to the wheels. For example, the ring gear can be locked into place so that the sun gear drives the planet carrier around. This increases power and reduces speed. The amount of turning power produced depends on the relative size of the gears in the set selected. There will be a gear set for low gear that will transfer much power but little speed to the wheels. There will be one or more gear sets for high gear that will transfer more speed but little power to the wheels.

If automatic transmissions sound complex, it's because they are. If they sound like they could be expensive to fix, it's because they can be. But they don't have to be. Here are a few ways to avoid problems with them.

Checking Automatic Transmission Fluid

To avoid premature wear, make sure your automatic transmission always has the correct level of transmission fluid. Transmissions are designed to work best with specific amounts of fluid. The amount and condition of this fluid determines the transmission's ability to change gears correctly; it creates the pressure needed to open and close valves and to fill and empty passageways. If there is insufficient fluid, the passageways won't fill correctly, the appropriate servos, bands, and clutches will not be activated, and the car will stay in one gear too long or it may not change gears at all.

Automatic transmission fluid also protects the transmission's delicate internal parts. Just as internal engine parts are subject to the laws of friction and wear, so are transmission parts: metal against metal causes friction,

friction causes heat, and heat causes wear. Transmission fluid acts as a lubricant, keeping hundreds of delicately machined internal parts from rubbing against each other by coating them with a thin film of oil.

Similar to engine oil, automatic transmission fluid is held in an oil pan bolted to the bottom of the transmission. A pump circulates it, and a transmission cooler (a radiator) keeps it from getting too hot. Check the fluid level or have it checked once a month. Your owner's manual tells you how to check the level in your particular car. Generally, the process goes like this. First, take your car for a short ride—no more than five minutes; now park the car, apply the emergency brake, and move the gear shift lever through all the gears P, N, D, and so on (make sure you hit them all). At this point, read your owner's manual to determine whether to put your car in Park or Neutral.

Now locate the dipstick (refer to your owner's manual). If you thought finding the engine oil dipstick was a job for Sherlock Holmes, you haven't seen anything yet! Having satisfied yourself that it is not the engine oil dipstick, pull it out, wipe it down, look at it, and return it to the tube from which it came. Make sure it is all the way back in. Pull it out again and note where the film line appears on the stick.

Although this procedure is similar to reading an engine oil dipstick, it takes a thorough review of your owner's manual and some practice to get it right. Just as you did in the case of the engine oil, if the transmission dipstick indicates that additional fluid is needed, be certain to use only the specific kind recommended in your manual. You will probably need a special funnel for adding fluid since the filler neck is very narrow. You can buy one in any auto parts store, or it may be easier to have your mechanic add the fluid. Most important, DO NOT OVERFILL.

Transmission fluid is a very lightweight oil, because it has to get between the delicate moving metal parts quickly to prevent damage. It should also be clear. If it is dark, has changed color noticeably, is filled with tiny pieces of metal and dirt, feels gritty, or has an unusual odor, reminding you of paint or varnish, it's probably a good time to have it checked out by a professional you trust.

Normally, discoloration of the fluid and deposits of metal filings are the result of overheating from abnormally hard use. You may have had to rock the car back and forth to get it out of a snow bank, or you may have driven up great mountains under heavy loads. But dirt and metal filings will accumulate inside any automatic transmission even if you don't abuse it. The solution may be to have your mechanic drain the system and refill with fresh fluid and a new filter.

The Automatic Transmission Filter

Yes, automatic transmissions have filters, too. Although a transmission filter doesn't look like most of the other filters, its job is equally important. It traps dirt and tiny metal fillings that naturally accumulate within the transmission body. If these particles get wedged among the delicate moving parts, they cause premature wear. If they lodge in the passageways, it won't be long before they block the flow of transmission fluid to one or more passageways. Such blockage will slow or stop the correct selection of gears. The gears may change harshly, erratically, slowly, not at the right time, or they may not change at all.

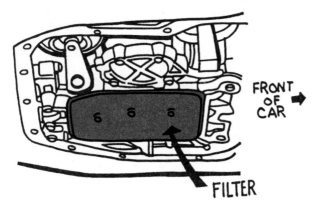

Transmission filters should be changed about every two years, even with normal use, or whenever your manual recommends. If a transmission has suffered unusual damage, the filter should be changed when the fluid is changed. This is not an expensive service, but it is a necessary one. Of all the regular maintenance items, this is the one most often overlooked.

Transmission TLC

If you want to avoid repair problems altogether, follow these simple rules. Do not put everything you need for a month in the country—four dogs, two cats, and your Nautilus equipment—in your car and drive cross-country or worse yet into the mountains. Carrying a heavy load, especially uphill, causes transmissions to work harder and get hotter. Overheating is a major cause of transmission damage. Cars have to carry heavy weights sometimes or they wouldn't be any good to you; however, if you want many, many healthy miles out of your transmission, leave the real load hauling to the professional shippers and movers. TLC for transmissions means limit the weight you carry on long trips, even if it means spending money on shipping.

Sometimes you have no choice. When you know the car will have a difficult task like lugging a heavy load up hill, use a lower gear. Those extra letters (1, 2, L, etc.) on the gear shift are not there just to fill up the empty slots. They allow you to take over temporarily as chief-in-charge of gear choice. Choosing a lower gear forces the transmission to stay in that lower gear until you change it back to automatic (Drive). Read your owner's manual for an explanation of how to use these gears. If it's not in there or you're still not comfortable with the procedure, ask a mechanic or a friend who knows something about cars to take a short ride with you and give you some coaching. Your transmission will appreciate it.

If you know that you're going to be traveling frequently with heavy loads (for example, towing a trailer in the mountains), consider having your car equipped with a special transmission cooler. It will act like an extra radiator, reduce potentially damaging high temperatures, and go a long way toward keeping your transmission young and healthy.

Accelerate slowly from a full stop. This will ensure many more miles of use before repairs or replacement of parts is necessary. Much transmission damage occurs in the morning, in the cold, before the transmission has had a chance to warm up and the fluid has been able to reach all the tiny openings that it must to protect the moving parts. Jumping in your car, throwing it in Reverse, and doing your impression of Mario Andretti at an Indy start as you

scream out of your driveway, trying to avoid missing that early appointment, is one sure way to pay for transmission work early and expensively.

If you are a runner, you wouldn't ask your body to run the 100-yard dash without warming it up. So don't ask your transmission to do that either. "Easy does it is" the rule. Give the car a minute or so to warm up (your engine will appreciate this kindness also) and then gently ease the car out of the driveway; wait until the car comes to a stop before you put it in Drive. For the first few miles, avoid sudden bursts of speed until everything down below is warmed up.

Transmission Adjustments and Repairs

Be aware of the specific recommendations of your owner's manual regarding transmission adjustments. As in manual transmissions, making sure that a professional performs all the adjustments necessary to accommodate the stretching and movement in the rods and levers that connect the transmission to the rest of the car will help extend its life dramatically. Lots and lots of basic work can usually be done by your regular mechanic or dealership, including maintenance and servicing, for example, adjusting linkage and external bands and changing the fluid, filter, and certain gaskets as well as some standard repairs.

Do not assume that transmission work will cost you a million dollars or your assumption may come true. If your transmission makes noises in cold weather only while it's warming up, and those noises go away as soon as it gets warm, it may be just suffering from the cold. But if the noises continue after the car is warm and running well, help may be needed.

If your transmission starts doing weird things like

growling, grinding, howling, scraping, clunking, or knocking, and it hasn't always made those sounds, it is probably a good time to have it checked. If it's slow to change gears, or it stays in one gear too long or won't change at all, first check the transmission fluid.

If the level is down, add the amount required and see if the symptom goes away. If not, or if the level was okay to begin with, have it looked at, but BE CAREFUL. Ask around and be certain that you check out the shop or the individual mechanic before letting anyone tear your transmission apart.

As with all repairs, if the car is still under warranty, be sure to take it to an authorized dealership. If it's not under warranty and you are using a franchise or independent shop, do your homework and get some references from people who have had work done by the particular shop. If the mechanics you normally use for engine and brake work don't work on transmissions, ask them who they use and how they rate their performance.

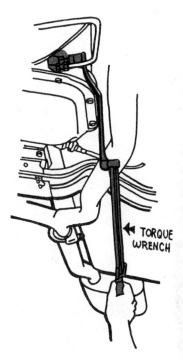

◄ TORQUE WRENCH

If you do not know the mechanic or shop well enough to trust them with your personal Swiss bank account number, ask for a written estimate in three-part form: disassemble, diagnose, and reassemble. You may want this written estimate even if you do trust them completely. I have always found that, whether I want a small carpentry job done or a sewing job or car repair, eliminating the unknowns goes a long way toward avoiding the problems that result from misunderstandings. What is said and what is heard can be very different. It's your responsibility as the consumer to protect yourself by clearing up any questions about price and what is included in that price in advance of the work.

If you don't like the diagnosis or feel the price is too high, or for some other reason you don't feel comfortable with the estimate and the eight million parts that make up your transmission are all over the mechanic's garage floor and you don't have an agreed price in writing to cover putting it back together again, you're not in a very good position to protect yourself from ripoff. You're stuck!

If you end up having major work done, remember to get a written guarantee. Ask the garage in advance whether they will give you one. If they don't guarantee their work,

"SOUNDS LIKE A LOT!"

consider going someplace else. If it looks as though extensive repair work is necessary, it may be worth looking into a rebuilt transmission backed by a good warranty. Rebuilding usually involves disassembly and replacement of bands, clutches, bushings, and seals as necessary.

Never be afraid to pick up your marbles and have the car towed somewhere else to get a second opinion. You may even need a special tow truck with a flatbed that keeps all four wheels off the ground while the car is being towed. Yes, it's inconvenient and, yes, it's going to cost more money; however, the savings of hundreds of dollars or more may make it worthwhile if the original diagnosis was inaccurate or unreasonable.

Final Drive: Continuing the Link of Power

We have so far traced the route of power from the engine to the transmission, which through its gears meets the changing power needs of the car by taking the speed of the engine and transferring it into sometimes powerful, sometimes speedy, sometimes zero turns of the transmission's output shaft. At this point, however, we still have a way to go to get this turning power to the car's wheels. For one thing, the transmission's output shaft is turning the wrong way (sideways), for another, the rotations are much too fast for the wheels (turning twice as fast as the latter should turn), and finally, when taking corners, the outside wheels of the car must travel farther and faster than the inside wheels. No, it's not done with mirrors, and your car has nothing up its sleeve, except some very special gears. Now we will follow it the final leg of its journey, sometimes called final drive, through the remainder of the drive train, from the transmission to the wheels.

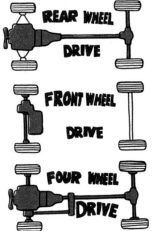

There are three distinct routes that it may take: rear-wheel drive, in which power is transferred to the car's rear wheels; front-wheel drive, in which power is transferred to the car's front wheels; and four-wheel drive—either part-time or full-time—in which power can be transferred to all four wheels. Each of these alternatives has advantages; each has disadvantages. When determining which system

offers the most benefits for you, think about where you live
and how and when you drive.

135

The Power Train

Rear-Wheel Drive

For many years, unless you drove a specialty vehicle, there
was only one power train to choose—rear-wheel drive. In
this method power's journey is from the transmission to
the car's rear wheels via a long turning bar or shaft, called
a driveshaft. (This shaft shows up inside the car in the
form of the hump in the floor between the driver's side and
the passenger's side.) Unfortunately, the motion that is
transferred from the transmission output shaft to the
driveshaft would have the car going down the road sideways—very convenient for parking, but no good for forward
progress.

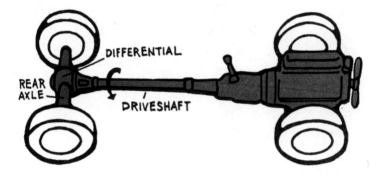

The Differential
Clearly, the motion of the driveshaft has to make a directional change. This change is made in the differential, a
specialized transmission. Here, a special set of gears called
the ring and pinion gear takes the turning motion of the
driveshaft and transfers it at a right angle to the rear axle,
a two-part shaft that joins the rear wheels. From there it's
smooth sailing to the wheels—well, almost.

There's still a small matter of the revolutions—they're
too fast. At 65 mph the driveshaft may be turning 5,000
times a minute. If that speed were transferred directly to
your car's wheels, you'd feel as though you were riding in a
rocket ship. Similar to the way transmissions cause gear
reductions, the differential gears now reduce the number

of driveshaft rotations. Consequently, the rotations of the wheels are now at a reasonable number. You might think changing direction and dramatically reducing speed would be plenty for any one system to handle, but the job of the differential is not over yet.

Do you remember what it was like as a kid to be the end skater on a "whip line." You'd be going so fast that your heart felt like it was coming out of your chest cavity and little gray hairs were popping out all over your other- wise youthful head, while the kid in the middle, wearing a malicious grin, would be practically standing still. Just as you were traveling farther and faster than any one else in the line, so the outside wheels of your car do as they pass

through corners. Another set of gears within the differen- tial divides the power of the engine between the two axle shafts so that the outside wheels can travel farther and faster than the inside wheels.

Since the differential is a specialized transmission, full of gears, it needs fluid to keep the gears from wearing prematurely. Differential fluid needs to be checked regu- larly to ensure it is at the correct level. Like transmission fluid, it doesn't usually evaporate, but a seal can break. The procedure for checking the differential fluid level is similar to that for manual transmission fluid. It is usually done by a professional when the car is on a lift, about once every six months or whenever your owner's manual recom- mends. If your differential requires a periodic fluid change, it will say so in your owner's manual. If no mention is made, the only time the fluid should be changed is if the differential has been damaged—generally through over- heating as a result of carrying a heavy load or being driven with the fluid level low.

From the differential, the power of the engine moves through the rear axleshafts to the rear wheels. There, at

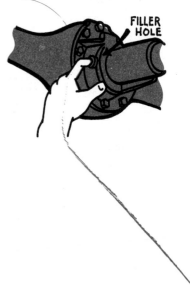

FILLER
HOLE

long last, the turning power of the engine becomes the forward or reverse motion of the car. This traditional rear-wheel-drive system has powered many cars for many miles and will continue to do so. Properly maintained, its major individual parts should last the lifetime of the car. But wherever two pieces of metal meet and continuously rub against each other, you can expect eventual wear. One of the places where two pieces of metal meet in the rear-wheel-drive system is at the universal joint, often referred to as a U-joint.

U-joints

U-joints are the wrists of a rear-wheel-drive car. Instead of bones, however, these metal connectors join and facilitate movement between the transmission output shaft and the driveshaft and the driveshaft and the differential. To see how U-joints work, keep your arm still and wave your hand up and down. The wrist motion is a simple flex, isn't it? Your hand is ideally designed with ligaments and muscles to help you perform this flexing motion many, many times without you're having to do anything to maintain it.

UNIVERSAL JOINT

HUMAN JOINT

Unlike the wrist, however, a U-joint needs special protection to perform its flexing motion without excess wear. A lubricant, in this case, a thick dark grease, bathes the joint to prevent metal from touching metal, thus keeping that old enemy friction, which translates into wear, at bay. Premature wear results in the eventual replacement of the U-joint.

On older cars, the U-joint is open and exposed to road dirt and contaminants. The grease that protects the joint also attracts dirt, and so it must be changed regularly. This procedure, called a "lube job," is usually done when the engine oil is changed but at an additional charge. The old grease is removed and clean grease is added.

U-joints are now usually sealed at the factory (as are most other joints, or places where two pieces of metal come together). While it's one less maintenance item for you to worry about, it's also one more component that you cannot get more miles out of with good maintenance—when it goes, it goes. Check with your mechanic to determine whether or not the U-joints on your car need to be lubed. If they do, be certain to check the bill to ensure that the procedure was done. You will also want any other joints, for example, the suspension and steering joints to be lubed at the same time (more about those in chap. 9).

Regardless of how U-joints are sealed or maintained, however, they move a lot and consequently wear out and may have to be replaced. A classic indication of a worn U-joint is a sound like two metal pots clanging together. If the windows are closed, these noises, which are particularly noticeable as the car is accelerating and decelerating, will sound more like a heavy thump-thump. Don't ignore its warning signs. A U-joint is not the world's most expensive item to replace, but if it actually breaks, the unrestrained twisting motion of the driveshaft can badly damage the undercarriage of your car. Not to mention stranding you wherever you are at that particular time.

Front-Wheel Drive

Although transferring the power of the engine to the front wheels, rather than the rear wheels, has been around for many, many years, it is only since the 1970s that front-wheel drive has been a popular alternative for passenger cars in the United States. Following the gas crunch in the 1970s, cars were designed to be lighter and smaller. Front-wheel drive offers a great advantage in that it concentrates the entire power train in the front of the car, where the weight of the engine provides excellent traction, while it leaves the rest of the car free for passengers and storage.

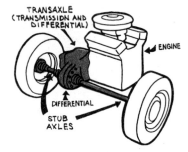

But front-wheel drive has its drawbacks also; for example, it's more complicated than rear-wheel drive. In rear-wheel drive, the path of the engine's turning power follows a straight line from the transmission, along the driveshaft, takes a right turn at the differential, and moves through the rear axle to the rear wheels. In a front-wheel-drive system, the engine's turning power follows a more convoluted path before it reaches the front wheels. The twists and turns this journey takes require more complicated components.

To begin with, there's no point keeping the differential between the rear wheels of the car anymore since power is no longer going there. The rear wheels now just follow along. The differential is moved forward between the front wheels where it is combined with the transmission into one unit called the transaxle. Instead of a long turning driveshaft leading to the rear axle, power in a front-wheel-drive system leaves the transmission section of the transaxle, turns around, and comes right back in to the differential section of the transaxle. It finally leaves the transaxle by way of the output shaft where it is joined to two shorter axles, called stub axles. These axles, which are connected to the front wheels, may be equal or unequal in length, depending on the position of the engine (whether it sits front to back or side to side).

CV Joints

Because the front wheels are also used for steering, the stub axles must be able to transfer the up-and-down motion of the road as well as the side-to-side motion of the steering. Consequently, the axles require a more complicated connector than the simple U-joint. Constant velocity joints, or CV joints, are the answer. To see how a CV joint works, hold your right elbow in your left palm and rotate it. Now compare that motion to the simple flexing motion of your wrist. The more complex the motion and the more

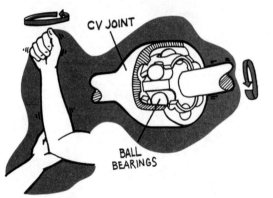

CV JOINT

BALL BEARINGS

complex the mechanism, the more expensive the mechanism is to build, repair, or replace. Therefore, CV joints deserve a little extra TLC if you want to avoid expensive repair bills.

Most important, the ball bearings inside the CV joints, which are responsible for the joint's more complex movement, are protected by rubber jackets called "boots." The CV joint is filled with lubricating grease and sealed to prevent contamination by dirt and other foreign matter. As long as the boots remain intact, the CV joints are protected.

You don't have to worry about CV joints, but you do need to have your mechanic check them regularly for damage whenever the car is up on a lift. It's a simple visual check that only takes a minute, but it's a minute that can save you hundreds of dollars. If the boot is cut or even slightly cracked, dirt quickly accumulates, contaminates the protective grease, and acts as an abrasive, causing a quick and dirty death to the joint. Make sure that this procedure is marked as completed on your repair bill or maintenance order.

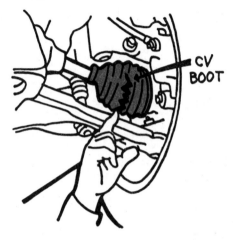

The demise of the CV joint is often indicated by a clicking sound coming from one of the front wheels, typically heard when the car is turning a corner. It doesn't take long to ruin the sensitive CV joint, so if you hear this warning sound, get to a professional and have the joints inspected for damage as soon as possible. If a minor tear in one of the boots is discovered, you may get away with a simple patch job: a silicone paste made especially for boot repair can be applied.

If a larger tear is discovered before dirt gets in and damages the joint (it doesn't take long), you may be able to simply install a boot "kit." This kit costs a lot less than replacing the entire CV joint. The rubber jacket is removed, clean grease is added, a new boot is installed, and the joint is sealed again.

Other than the normal wear and tear experienced by any metal objects that move a lot, the CV joint should remain trouble-free. But keep in mind that a tear can occur accidentally if the car runs over a sharp object. So be alert to that possibility, and don't test drive your car like they do on TV—up mountains, through rivers, and so on.

Four-Wheel Drive

Although at one time four-wheel drive was reserved for heavy-duty utility vehicles, in recent years the technology that transfers power to all four wheels has developed to the point where there is a whole generation of four-wheel-drive passenger cars and light trucks from which to choose. Not only are there many manufacturers designing four-wheel-drive cars but they are doing it in very different ways.

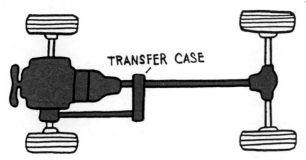

Traditional part-time, four-wheel drive transfers power either to the rear or front wheels through a rear and front differential. It can also transfer power to all four wheels through what's called a transfer case. This special third set of gears, which sits between the two driveshafts leading to the two differentials, locks the front and rear axles together. When power is transferred to all four wheels, instead of just the front two or just the rear two, a car on a slippery road gets tons of traction.

On earlier models, it was necessary to climb out of the vehicle and turn the locks on the wheel hubs manually in order to lock the front and rear wheels together for traveling on slippery road surfaces. When dry roads reappeared it was necessary to climb out and unlock the hubs. Driving a part-time four-wheel-drive vehicle with the axles locked on dry pavement resulted in damage to the power train. Front and rear wheels need to turn at slightly different speeds as they go through corners. When the axles are locked together, they are forced to turn at the same speed.

On wet roads, the tires compensate by slipping a little, but on dry roads, the strain from having to turn together can damage the drive train. This "wind up" is why on part-time four-wheel-drive cars, the four wheels are engaged only when the car is on ice, snow, mud or other uneven surfaces, never on dry pavement.

Most part-time four-wheel-drive vehicles today have an interior shift lever to make locking and unlocking hubs easy and convenient. To make them even more convenient, a number of systems have been developed which take the decision to engage all four wheels away from the driver and make it an automatic function. While the technology of these "on-demand" four-wheel-drive systems is still in a development stage, a number of options are already available, and we can expect to see many more in the future.

On-Demand Four-Wheel Drive

Among the variations of on-demand four-wheel drive is a system that connects the front and rear axles by means of metal plates attached to each, which are then bathed in a special coupling fluid. Under normal driving conditions, the plates are not connected. Power flows to one axle only as it would in any front- or rear-wheel-drive car. But if one wheel loses traction and starts spinning, the temperature of the coupling fluid changes and it thickens. The thickened fluid locks the two metal plates and also locks the two axles together. With both axles "live," all four wheels are now receiving power. Unless you're buried up to your eyeballs in mud or snow, the car should be able to get enough traction to move.

In this way, when the car needs extra traction all four wheels are automatically in service. When the car returns to dry pavement, the good traction sends a signal to the

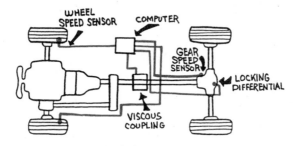

fluid, the temperature of which changes back to normal, and the plates relax and disconnect.

A computer-assisted version for two wheel drive which will have sensors that will feed back information about traction to a computer that will then transfer or back off power as needed is also on the drawing boards.

Whichever power train you choose, your decision should be guided by your own needs. Look first at the road conditions where you travel most frequently. Is the terrain hilly and the roads steep and winding? Do they look more like goat paths than highways? Or is the surrounding area flat with gentle rolling countryside. What's the normal weather pattern? Are there frequent and heavy snowfalls or bad ice storms? Is spring synonymous with mud? If you need the extra traction that either front-wheel-drive or four-wheel-drive systems offer, then that's where you should begin to investigate. Keep in mind, however, the differences that exist in the average annual maintenance cost among these vastly different vehicles. You can find that information in *Consumer Reports*, which is updated yearly. Many manufacturers offer cars in each category so you will find no shortage of vehicles to choose from.

9

Steering and Suspension

Now that we have this 2,500-pound-plus hunk of metal and rubber moving swiftly and powerfully down the road, we need a device for aiming it in the right direction. At plus or minus 100 to 200 pounds of muscle and bone, you're not likely to do that without some help. Your car's steering system supplies that help—making the car go in the direction you want it to go is as easy as tearing the top off your cereal box, easier, in fact.

Steering and suspension are kindred spirits. If steering is about controlling the right, left, and straight directional movement of your car, then suspension is about controlling its up and down movement as it travels over the uneven road surface. These two systems not only share some of the same components but they both contribute to each other's performance and to your control of the car as it travels down the highway. Consequently, we'll cover them both in this chapter.

SHOCK ABSORBER

REAR LEAF SPRINGS

FRONT COIL SPRINGS

SUSPENSION

STEERING

Before modern-day steering mechanisms were invented, cars were steered by a stick similar to the tiller found on a sailboat. By the turn of the century, however, the earliest models for today's systems had been introduced: a combination of rods, levers, and gears replaced tillers, improving both the accuracy of the steering system and the maneuverability of the car.

Today, there are basically two types of steering systems available for most cars: traditional or rack and pinion. For most passenger cars, both these systems operate in conjunction with the front wheels only. We'll look at four-wheel steering, an increasingly popular system that operates with both front and rear wheels, and its advantages and disadvantages later in this chapter, but for now we'll concentrate on steering that is limited to the front wheels.

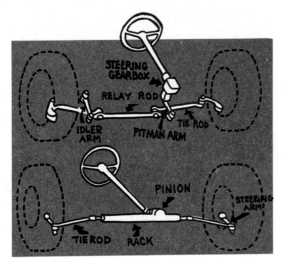

Traditional Steering Systems

In traditional steering systems, a steering wheel is attached to a steering shaft that sits inside a tube called the steering column. As the driver rotates the steering wheel clockwise or counterclockwise, the rotational movement is transferred down the shaft to a steering gearbox. This gearbox, another specialized transmission, not only changes the steering wheel's direction but also multiplies its turning power. In combination with a series of connecting rods and levers, steering gears convert the circular motion of the steering column into the side-to-side motion of the wheels; consequently, the wheels point right, left, or straight. In addition, like all their toothed cousins—transmission gears, differential gears—steering gears multiply turning power. The force you exert on the steering wheel is magnified many, many times, thus making the herculean task of maneuvering your car easy—almost.

While the gears inside a traditional steering box may differ in style from one car to another, they all need to be bathed in fluid to prevent metal-to-metal contact, the familiar friction, heat, and wear scenario.

Rack and Pinion Steering

Rack and pinion may sound like a new method of medieval torture, but it's really a popular compact and lightweight steering mechanism that works particularly well with smaller front-wheel-drive cars where space and weight are a major consideration. Rack and pinion steering eliminates the traditional steering gearbox and replaces it with a simpler set of gears: a toothed wheel called a pinion gear is attached to the end of the steering shaft where it meets

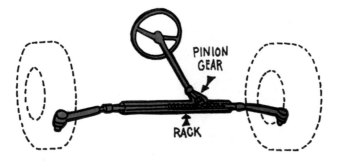

PINION
GEAR

RACK

a long bar or rack that also has teeth. Rods and levers called tie rods and steering arms attach the rack to the wheels, which themselves spin on a tapered rod called the steering spindle. As the steering wheel turns clockwise or counterclockwise, the pinion gear rotates along the rack causing the rack to move right or left and the front wheels of the car to turn right or left.

Rack and pinion steering systems are precise. They're also more expensive to repair than traditional steering components because the entire rack assembly, rather than a simple rod or lever, may have to be replaced.

Steering System Maintenance and Wear

Theoretically, steering gears generally don't wear out. In traditional steering systems, the level of the steering gear fluid inside the gearbox should remain constant since there is little heat to evaporate the fluid and the steering gearbox is sealed. Some manufacturers require a periodic check of the fluid level by a professional and provide a filler hole for this inspection. Other manufacturers do not. Your owner's manual tells whether or not a check is necessary and what kind of fluid to add if it is. But just as any container's rubber seals can shrink or break, so can the seals for the steering gearbox. If the steering system is being serviced according to the recommendations in your owner's manual, and you're keeping an eye out for leaks under the car, you should know about a leak long before damage could be done to the gears. If a leak does occur, have it repaired and the fluid replaced immediately.

Rack and pinion systems are sealed with protective boots, so unless the seal breaks, these gears should also remain trouble-free. The problem is, they don't. Seals shrink and crack as they age, especially in very cold weather. If the rack is exposed to the ravages of dust and dirt, wears quickly. Making sure those boots are visually and carefully inspected every time your car is on a lift will go a long way to ensuring their extended health.

Adequate lubrication should keep steering gears from premature wear, but the linkage—the rods and levers that connect the steering gears to the wheels—ordinarily wear with use and will eventually need adjustment as it stretches with age. In traditional steering, system linkage includes the pitman arm, idler arm, relay rod, tie rods, and steering arms; in rack and pinion steering, it includes tie rods and steering arms. Even more wear occurs where the action is, at the joints, the tie rod ends, which connect the rods and levers. Just as the joints in the human body— elbows and knees—wear more than the bones themselves, so do the joints of the steering system.

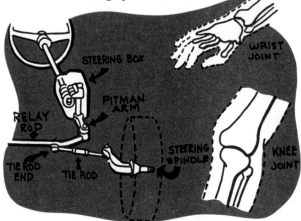

When steering linkage and joints wear, more motion or play comes into the steering wheel. The feeling in the steering wheel is no longer as firm and tight as it was when the car was new or newer. Your feeling of connection won't be as sure, and the steering wheel may even feel loose or sloppy. The car, with you in it, should track nice and straight down the road without your having to adjust the position of the steering wheel constantly to keep the car on course. If when you turn the steering wheel the road wheels are slow to respond, there is too much play in the steering. Have it checked by a professional as soon as possible.

To keep repair costs at a minimum, about once a year or whenever your owner's manual recommends, have the entire steering system checked and adjusted if necessary. The extent of steering component wear is normally determined by a professional manually holding the rods and levers and shaking them to see how much they move. Remember that all joints will move some when you grab and tug at them—even when they're brand spanking new. Be sure that you get a second opinion if you're not completely convinced that the diagnosis is appropriate and the price is fair.

Limited adjustments to the system as it wears extend its useful life many thousands of miles. Rack and pinion systems can be adjusted but not as easily as traditional gearboxes, and maintenance is not typically required as it is for traditional steering. Check your owner's manual for specifications. On newer cars, tie rod ends and most other joints are sealed at the factory.

Power Steering

In the early days, cars ran on very narrow tires and were extremely responsive to the least guidance from the steering wheel. Driving these cars may have been easy on the driver's arms but not so on their legs, for the driver and passengers often walked home after the car skittered off the road. To be up close and personal with ditches was not a desired condition, but it was a frequent one.

With the introduction and acceptance of fatter tires, this excessive responsiveness was diminished. Fat tires kept vehicles on the road better, but they made it more difficult to park in small spaces. Parking a car weighing over 3,000 pounds became a chore fit for a weightlifter. The answer was to add the turning power of the engine to the already formidable turning power of the steering gears. Voila! Power steering.

Whether it is incorporated in the steering gearbox (integral power steering) or added onto the system afterward by affecting the linkage outside the gears, power steering makes it easier to turn the car at slow speeds. This added assistance, which can be added to both traditional and rack and pinion steering, comes from a power steering pump run by a belt powered by the car's engine. This pump puts pressure on the power steering fluid,

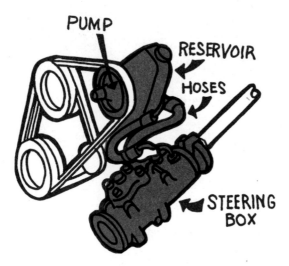

PUMP

RESERVOIR

HOSES

STEERING BOX

which is held in a reservoir. Fluid pressure is put on the steering gears to increase turning power and to change direction. Consequently, less manual pressure is needed to turn the steering wheel.

If the belt for the pump breaks or the fluid in the reservoir is too low to function properly, the power assist is lost. You will still be able to steer, but you'll have to really crank on that steering wheel to get the same reaction from the wheels that your little finger obtained for you earlier. "Muscle steering" is no fun and can be downright scary, so check the power steering fluid level in the reservoir regularly, or have it checked (about once a month) and top it off when necessary. The dipstick is often located under the cap of the pump. Since the steering system is not subjected to much heat, the fluid should not be disappearing regularly. If every time you check the dipstick you have to top it off, there's a good chance that there's a leak in the system somewhere. Have it checked by a professional.

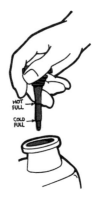

When adding fluid, check the specification in your owner's manual. It used to be that power steering and automatic transmission fluids were interchangeable, but most manufacturers now specify special fluids. Sorry, substitutions off this menu can cause serious malfunction problems as well as a possible voiding of the warranty.

One side effect of power assist is to change the feel of the wheel and your sense of connection to the road. Manufacturers are now adding sensors that electronically read the speed of the wheels and reduce the power assist to the steering function when you're traveling at highway speeds, where the extra boost is not needed, and reinstate it when you're traveling at slower speeds. This makes it easy to park without losing that good road feel when driving.

Four-Wheel Steering

While only the front wheels usually steer, four-wheel steering has been around for many years, but only recently has it become attractive to modern automotive engineers. It is desirable to have a system for the back wheels similar to that for the front, because there is always some delay in transferring the turning motion of the steering wheels to the traditional directionally fixed rear wheels. This delay is referred to as "drag" and is especially true when cornering. Remember that in chapter 9 we discussed how

momentum causes a car to want to continue in a straight line unless a greater force interferes? This is also true when your car goes through a corner. It really wants to continue in a straight direction. It is the traction (adhesion to the road) provided by the front tires which enables the car to continue through the corner, helping it to stay on the course that the steering wheel has directed, even though the rear wheels actually experience drag in a straight direction.

In four-wheel steering at high speeds, the rear wheels are directed through the turn at the same angle, at the same time as the front wheels are. The delay and drag usually felt by the rear wheels is gone. This provides more force through the completion of the turn and works against the tendency of the car to continue straight. The car gains a higher degree of maneuverability, especially in high speed cornering and lane changing.

At low speeds and particularly when the front wheels

are turned at a sharp angle, as in parking maneuvers, the rear wheels move in the opposite direction of the front wheels. This makes parallel parking of the biggest sedan as easy as parking the smallest compact.

To accomplish this bit of trickery, manufacturers of current four-wheel steering systems use two methods. One employs a second steering gearbox mechanically linked to the front wheel steering gearbox and to the rear wheels. The other method employs two different steering gear systems whose motion is coordinated electronically by a computer.

Whether you want to pay the additional cost these systems now add to the base price of a car is the question. For effortless parking, four-wheel steering is the greatest. For high speed maneuverability, some manufacturers maintain that a good suspension system will accomplish the same results for less money.

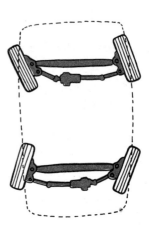

Suspension

If steering is about controlling the right, left, and straight directional movement of your car, then suspension is about controlling its up and down movement, specifically, the up and down motion that results because the body of your car is suspended over its frame as it rolls down the road on four cushioned, round rubber feet.

We tend to think of the suspension as the system that gives us a nice comfortable ride. And it's true. Were it not for your car's suspension, every time you went over a bump, the car would bounce, and bounce, and bounce. Ad

SHOCK ABSORBER

REAR LEAF SPRINGS

FRONT COIL SPRINGS

SUSPENSION

nauseam. But it's far more important to your safety than comfort. The suspension components affect steering and braking and keep the tires of the car firmly planted on the road so you stay in control. That's why it's worth a closer look to determine whether the suspension system in your car is up to par.

Future computer-controlled suspensions that could have cars walking up stairs may not resemble the suspensions of today's cars, but their objectives will be the same: to provide passengers with the most comfortable ride and the best possible road handling. The majority of today's car manufacturers use similar suspension components—springs, shock absorbers, struts, and metal arms—combining them in various sizes and shapes in both the front and the rear of the car.

Comfort and Control

Most cars today have independent suspension, both front and rear. Independent suspension is just that—independent. Each wheel responds independently to changes in the surface of the road.

FIXED SUSPENSION

The difference between the front and rear suspension components is largely determined by their job. Since the rear wheels don't steer, they have fewer angles to contend with. However, the amount of weight that has to be distributed properly by the rear suspension varies more than it does for the front; and in rear-wheel-drive cars, the rear also has to transfer the turning power of the engine.

Each wheel is attached to the frame of the car by metal arms called control arms. The name of each is determined by its shape and its location (upper/lower). For example, A-arms are made in the triangular shape of the letter A. A wishbone is made in the shape of a wishbone. A control arm may be upper, lower, or trailing (i.e., it may trail behind the frame or cross member). Control arms rarely wear out. The single exception to this rule is when, as is the case with some imports, the ball joint (a tie rod end's big brother) is part of the lower control arm. If, however, a control arm is damaged by impact, it can bend or break.

Ball Joints, Bushings, and Wheel Bearings

Just as with the steering system, it is the suspension's connecting joints, ball joints, that wear. An integral part of both the steering and the suspension, ball joints allow the steering components to move up and down as well as side to side, compensating for uneven road surfaces. As ball joints wear, the feeling you might experience as you drive is a feeling of sloppiness or looseness in the steering. Ball joint wear in older cars is usually determined by the amount of movement in the wheel when the car is on a lift. On many newer cars, it's less of a guessing game: ball joints have a ring or collar, which moves in a downward motion from its original position as the joint wears, indicating the need for replacement. If replacement is recommended, ask the mechanic what method is being used to determine wear. In any case, ask for the old part(s) back.

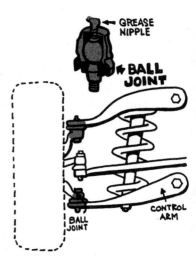

The ball joints on newer cars are often sealed at the factory, so you don't have to worry about them. If your car

has the older type, however, they must be regularly maintained with a periodic lube; the old grease is removed and replaced with clean new grease through a grease fitting. As with tie rod ends, this procedure is done when the engine oil is changed and is the part of the lube job discussed in chapter 9. Ask your mechanic which type your car has, and if it's the type that must be lubed, check the bill each time to be sure the procedure has been done.

If damage or wear occurs to either a control arm or a joint, the angle at which the wheel meets the road will be affected. Whenever that angle strays from manufacturer's specifications you'll want to have it corrected ASAP. An incorrect angle means incorrect alignment, which adversely affects both road handling and tire wear. More about alignment in chapter 12.

One other suspension part that you may eventually need to have replaced during the lifetime of your car is a bushing. This metal or rubber liner helps to reduce wear between two parts by acting as a cushion. Bushings are not restricted to the suspension but are found throughout the car. The cost of the bushing is incidental; the real cost will be in the time it takes to pull the component apart which the bushing serves and put it back together. Some components are quick and easy to reach, some are not. Make sure your estimate indicates how much the part costs and how much the labor is and then check around to see if the quoted price is reasonable.

Because wheel bearings, when they wear, will often produce symptoms similar to those of worn steering and suspension components (they will also produce symptoms similar to worn brake components), we'll cover them here. To explain what wheel bearings are I have to begin with a question. Have you ever stepped on a golf ball? Ever step on a bunch of golf balls? Ever step on a board on top of a bunch of golf balls? Then you already know quite a lot about wheel bearings.

Wheel bearings resemble metal doughnuts with many tiny steel balls, called ball bearings, inside. They have outer and inner rings called races. They function just as all bearings do, by distributing the weight and turning force of another object. In this case, the object is the axle shaft. They are found where the axle joins the wheel. Like other

places in the car where two pieces of metal come together, wheel bearings are packed with grease which provides a lubricating cushion and separates metal from metal. By having the axle shaft rotate inside the wheel bearing the ball bearings are able to help distribute the weight of the axle evenly so that as the shaft turns, it experiences less pressure and therefore less wear.

Wheel bearings not only extend the life of the axle but they also contribute significantly to proper road handling through smooth steering and braking. In older model cars, wheel bearings are removed periodically and repacked with clean grease to extend the life of the working parts. On newer cars, wheel bearings are often sealed at the factory. If they wear they are replaced as a unit.

Springs

Before the days of rubber tires, wagons carrying passengers and freight guaranteed a very hard ride to all participants. Every bump from every rock and uneven bit of roadway was transferred directly through the wheels to the seats and benches. With the development of rubber tires, things improved greatly.

The air-filled rubber tires surrounded the wheels and cushioned the passenger from road surface irregularities, but they also generated a lot of unwanted "bounce for the ounce," which was transferred to the vehicle. To isolate the passenger from this movement, different types of springs were developed. Springs compress to absorb the motion of the wheels hitting a bump and extend to release the motion when the car passes to level ground.

There are three main types of springs used for absorbing motion in passenger vehicles: coil springs, leaf springs, and torsion bars. Coil springs, the most common ones in use today on passenger cars, are incorporated in both front and rear suspensions. They are attached to the frame of

the car and look a lot like old bed springs or oversized metal slinkies as they compress and extend again and again (in response to the irregularities in the road surface), before returning to their original shape.

Leaf springs absorb the motion of the wheels as the uneven strips of metal of which they're made flatten and unflatten. These leaves are tied together by bolts and clips. They are still found on many four-wheel-drive vehicles and in the rear of light trucks and some domestic passenger cars. Torsion bars absorb the road motion by means of a bar that twists and turns as the motion is received.

If a spring is worn or breaks, you will either feel, see, or hear a difference. The ride will become rough, to say the least. The car may pull to one side as you brake. As you look at the car from the front or rear, one corner will generally appear lower than the other. You may hear the sound of metal clanging against metal coming from underneath the car—great roaring thuds every time you go over a bump.

Be careful, however. If your car is a lightweight model, it may normally make weird noises simply because its suspension is not as beefy as the suspension in a heavier car. If this is a problem for your car, you may want to upgrade the quality of the springs with variable-rate springs, which provide additional stiffness to the suspension when the car is carrying a heavy load but will not give you the harsher ride that installing a simple heavier spring would.

Shock Absorbers

Any type of spring would keep compressing and extending until we got seasick if it were not for shock absorbers, which work like a door closure, the kind with the metal tube that allows the door to open freely and close slowly. By absorbing some of the motion, the fluid in the door closure controls the speed at which the door returns to its original position. In a similar way, the shock absorber reduces the up-and-down movement transmitted by the spring.

SHOCK ABSORBER

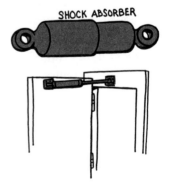

Like the door closure, the shock absorber is a sealed system filled with fluid; it contains two tubes that share a common center and a piston. This piston is located inside the inner tube and has tiny openings or valves that allow fluid to pass in and out. The piston moves up and down faster if the openings are larger, and the ride is then smoother; the piston moves up and down more slowly if the openings are made smaller, and the ride is then harsher. The top of the shock absorber tube is attached to the frame of the car; the bottom is attached to a suspension arm. As the car moves up and down, the fluid is pushed through the tiny openings, allowing the piston to move up and down faster or slower (depending on the size of the openings), thus limiting or reducing the motion of the compressing and extending spring. It is this reduction of movement in the shock absorber that determines how much up-and-down motion is transferred to the passenger compartment and, consequently, the smoothness or harshness of the ride.

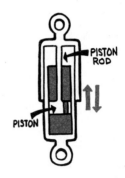

A variety of different kinds of absorbers have been developed in recent years for the purpose of giving passengers the most comfortable ride, with the greatest control, and under a variety of different load conditions. For most passenger vehicles, which do not tow trailers or carry the entire little league team in the rear of the car every day, regular old shock absorbers work just fine. After a heavy workout, however, any regular shock absorber is prone to "fading."

Fading occurs when a shock absorber works too hard, for example, riding on very rough unpaved roads. In response to this excessive demand, one tube moves rapidly and continuously inside the other, causing foam or air bubbles to form inside the tubes. These air spaces reduce the efficiency of the fluid to absorb the movement and the shock absorber becomes less efficient temporarily. The quality of the ride is consequently diminished, and endless bouncing takes place even if the shocks are new and in good working order. The air in the fluid inhibits the shocks from doing their job. Gas-charged shocks were developed as one response to this problem.

Gas-powered shocks, which are becoming standard on many newer models, use a nitrogen charge to pressurize the fluid in the piston. Under pressure, air bubbles can't form. The shock absorbers maintain a steady performance, providing a smoother ride, regardless of the difficulty or the unfriendliness of the terrain.

Heavy-duty shocks are regular shock absorbers but larger in size and with more fluid. The more fluid, the more motion the shock can absorb. The loads a heavy-duty shock absorber can handle are greater and the wheels stay planted firmly on the ground, but the ride is harsher. These replacement shocks are worth considering if your car frequently carries heavy weights.

If your car frequently carries dramatically different weights at different times, you might want to consider a variable load shock. Either mechanically or electronically (by computer), the shock absorber is instructed to respond differently to various weights carried in the car. The variable load shock does this by first sensing a change in weight. It then changes the size of the piston's openings: larger and the ride is smoother, smaller and the ride is harsher.

MacPherson Struts

Another variation from the traditional shock absorber is the MacPherson strut. It enjoys overwhelming popularity among manufacturers of front-wheel-drive cars, because it combines some of the traditional suspension components and eliminates others to make a smaller, lighter, more compact unit.

MAC PHERSON STRUT

MacPherson struts have eliminated the upper control arm that traditionally attached the wheel to the frame and created a nice cozy collar on which to rest the spring and shock absorber. By combining the spring and shock absorber into one unit and replacing the upper control arm with a metal bar or strut, the latter now acts as part of the suspension link. The shock absorber sits inside the strut and a collar or flange is added to the strut so that the spring can rest on the collar. The strut now acts as the upper control arm once did and connects the unit to the frame of the car.

Getting rid of the upper control arm by replacing it with the strut also limits the amount of variation in the angle of the tires as they respond to irregularities in the road surface. With less change in the angle of the tire, there is greater stability and improved road handling, which is why MacPherson struts are believed to be superior to many earlier types in which the shock and the spring acted through separate upper and lower control arms.

Depending on the quality of shock absorbers in your car, the kind of driving you do, the loads your car carries, and the terrain over which you drive, shock absorbers do wear out and will probably need to be replaced (always in pairs) in your car at least once during its lifetime. Since they combine the shock absorber, spring, and suspension arm, MacPherson struts are more complicated and more expensive to replace. Sometimes, however, just the shock absorber component can be replaced, which reduces the cost substantially. When the time comes for replacement, ask your mechanic whether partial replacement is a possibility for the MacPherson struts in your car before you have the entire unit replaced. The costs involved depend to a large extent on how the strut is attached to the lower suspension arm. The form of attachment determines the ease (or lack of) with which the strut can be reached.

A worn shock absorber or strut, no matter what type it is, is evident in the feel of the car. You may notice more bounce than you did when the car was new or newer, or the car will dip forward in the front dramatically with hard braking. If you step down on one side of the bumper and then release it and the car continues to bounce up and down more than three times, you probably have a worn shock absorber. You may, if you happen to be crawling around under you car, see some dark fluid on the outside of the shock absorber. The presence of fluid indicates a leak. Tire wear patterns that show scalloping or cupping will eventually appear as well.

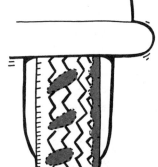

More recently, we are being told by manufacturers and replacement experts that a more sophisticated diagnosis is required than the feel and the look of the car and that only the "experts" can decide when replacement of the shock absorber is appropriate. As with all the other systems in your car, the suspension and steering should be maintained and repaired by a professional whom you trust. Front end work, which lumps all these together, has traditionally been an area of high consumer dissatisfaction. If the replacement of steering or suspension components is called for, be sure to call around to different shops before you commit to having the work done. See what the price ranges are, and as always, be sure you get a complete list of what's included for the price.

In addition, whenever you're looking at suspension features in relation to buying a car, evaluate first your own driving needs. Be sure that you need the super-duper and more expensive suspension before you pay for it. If you're a speed limit highway driver, you may be buying a feature that you will never take advantage of unless you somehow get to run at Indianapolis.

10

Brakes

Now that we've got all this metal and rubber rolling down the road in the right direction, its high time we figured out how to stop it! Of all the systems that contribute to your safety, this is probably the most important.

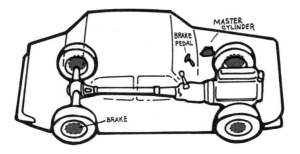

Brakes work on the principle that fluids cannot be compressed. Put any fluid in an airtight container, push on it, and the fluid will push on something else. Unlike the gas and air that compressed very cooperatively in the combustion chambers of the engine, brake fluid will not compress.

Brake fluid is stored in a metal or plastic reservoir called a master cylinder. To ensure that there will always be some breaking action, the master cylinder is divided into two separate sections. Each section activates a different pair of brakes. If there's a leak in the system, a valve seals off the malfunctioning system from the healthy system. Theoretically, you should always have one set of working brakes. One is supposed to do you, but if you have ever had one set of brakes go out, you know that the results are

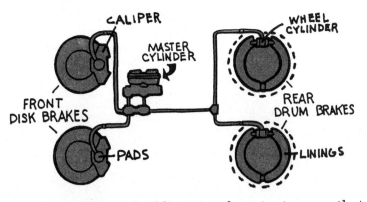

less than confidence building—you have to stomp on that brake pedal to get the car to stop!

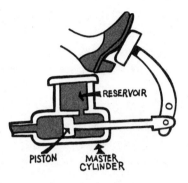

When you push on the brake pedal, brake fluid is forced out of the master cylinder along two different sets of brake lines to the two separate sets of brakes. The typical system today is made up of two different types of brakes that work in unison. Disc brakes are generally found in the front and drum brakes in the rear. Today, however, more cars are showing up with disc brakes all the way around. We'll get to the reasons for this change later on.

Drum Brakes

Let's begin with drum brakes. A metal canister with the top cut off is attached to the turning wheel. Inside are two crescent-shaped "shoes" to which linings are glued (bonded) or nailed (riveted). The linings are similar in composition to the friction or sneaker-type material that lines the clutch disc, as we discussed in chapter 8.

The shoes are attached to a metal backing plate that holds these and the other working parts of the brake. Between the two shoes is a wheel cylinder, which is a tiny version of the hollow metal tube that makes up the compression chambers located in the engine. Each wheel cylinder contains two pistons or arms, again smaller versions of the round metal plugs that went up and down in the engine.

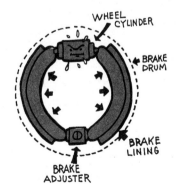

When you push on the brake pedal, brake fluid is forced out of the master cylinder reservoir, passes through the brake lines, and fills the wheel cylinder to capacity, which forces the pistons out from either side of the cylinder. As the pistons push out against the shoes, the linings come in contact with the inside of the rolling brake drum. The friction that results as the sneakertype material pushes against the drum causes the wheel to slow and eventually stop. When the brake is released, the fluid returns to the reservoir, and miniature coil springs, called return springs, bring the shoes back into their original positions. The shoes remain in this retracted position, attached to the backing plate and rolling along with the drum until the pedal is pushed again.

Each time the linings are forced against the inside of the drum, friction and heat result. The old friction, heat, wear rule takes over and the linings gradually wear. As they do, they naturally become thinner, causing the brake shoe to travel farther to make contact with the inside of the turning drum. Braking action gradually diminishes. To compensate for the worn linings, you have to push harder on the pedal to stop the car. The brake pedal will feel less sharp, less crisp. A brake adjustment is required to remedy this situation.

If your brakes are self-adjusting (as most newer brakes are), you can adjust them yourself. When you begin to notice a slight reduction in braking, find a safe spot, put the car in reverse, and step on the brake fairly hard. If you do this a few times, the self-adjusting screw should take the slack resulting from the worn lining. Isn't it nice to know there are still some Do-It-Yourself procedures left?

If you don't know whether your brakes are self-adjusting or not, look in your owner's manual or ask your mechanic. In any case, if your brakes haven't been examined by a professional in a while (perhaps over a year), or you don't know when they were serviced last, make an appointment as soon as you can to determine the status of their health. Guesswork in this area is a no-brainer.

If you discover that your brakes are not self-adjusting, a mechanic can take up the slack by moving the linings closer to the drum, until the linings are so worn that they require replacement. Linings, by the way, are no longer made of asbestos (thanks to the EPA) but of fiberglass or tiny slivers of metal and other materials compressed together. These composition linings are harder than asbestos and have excellent friction qualities for performing the old sneaker trick.

Brake drum linings should be replaced regularly. If they aren't, the friction material will wear so thin that the harder metal surface of the shoe, or the metal rivets that attach the lining to the shoe, will come in contact with the smooth surface of the inside of the drum and scratch it.

A drum break will usually tell you when it's in trouble. You'll hear a metal grinding sound coming from the rear of the car as you brake. It is the sound made by the shoe or the rivets as they scratch the inside of the turning drum. The drum may have to be removed and the upper layer of metal shaved off by a special machine (lathe) to make the surface smooth again. A smooth, even surface is essential

if the lining is to work properly. If the scratching goes on too long, and the scratches are very deep, the drum itself may become thin, too thin to absorb the heat that the friction action of braking causes. You may need to buy a new set of drums. (Brakes, no matter what kind, are always replaced in pairs.)

Like most other moving parts of the car, wheel cylinders also wear eventually. Wheel cylinder failure may result in the pistons not retracting correctly after braking and the linings being constantly forced against the inside of the drum. The brakes are said to be "hung up," and the result is abnormal wear to the lining. A brake that gets hung up may cause the car to pull to one side or you may detect a burning odor or smoke as the lining fries merrily away.

The wheel cylinder seal that contains the oil, which keeps the piston lubricated, may leak onto the linings, causing them to swell. The brakes may then pull to one

side (grab), or the brake pedal may pulse (push back errati- cally) or feel bumpy as it is depressed.

Disc Brakes

Disc brakes use the same principle as drum brakes for slowing or stopping but different mechanisms. A caliper, a metal fist with one or two fingers (pistons) in it, is attached to a pair of kidney-shaped brake pads lined with friction material. In between these two pads sits a metal frisbee or disc called a rotor, which is connected to the turning wheel. When the brakes are applied, the brake fluid is again forced out of the master cylinder, where it passes through the brake linings to the caliper. There the fluid forces the pistons to squeeze the pads together, clamping them against the turning rotor and creating the friction that causes the rotor to slow and eventually stop.

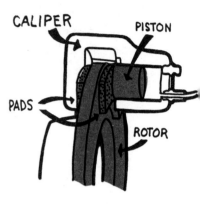

After a while, the linings wear down and the metal rivets or the plates to which they are bonded make metal-to-metal contact and scratch the surface of the rotor. If the scratches are not too deep, the rotor is removed and put on a lathe, and the top surfaces are ground down to make the rotor smooth again. As is true for the brake drums, if the scratches are so deep that removing them would leave too little metal on the rotor to absorb heat properly, you'll wind up having them replaced at a much higher cost than a simple brake pad replacement.

The sound you might hear from a worn brake pad in metal-to-metal contact is a squealing or squeaking coming from the front of the car when you apply the brakes. The trouble is that squealing, squeaking brakes may also be caused by loose parts (pads that are not snug enough and are vibrating against the rotor) or by dirt that has become trapped in them. Worse yet, some brakes squeak when it's hot, some squeak when it's cold, some squeak when it's wet, some squeak when it's dry, and some brakes just plain squeak.

When asbestos pads were replaced by metal composition pads, the pads got much harder. The hard rotor rubbing against the harder pad can cause a squeaking sound similar to chalk on a blackboard. If you're hearing this sound and it's making you crazy, especially if you're hearing it in a new car or from a brand-new set of brake pads, ask your mechanic whether applying a silicone compound directly to the brake pads or beveling (rounding) the edges of the pads so they are not as sharp will alleviate this irritating noise. Unfortunately, sometimes you'll be told that you just have to live with it or replace the pad with a softer (probably cheaper) type, which usually wears faster. Now there's a trade-off!

Another sound that you may hear coming from your brakes is a chirp. If you hear a chirping noise coming from the front wheels, not when you're braking but when the car is moving, it is probably a "wear indicator," a small piece of soft metal positioned so that it touches the surface of the rotor when the pad is ready to be replaced. It's saying, "Hey there! Your brake pads are low. Replace them now, before a routine maintenance item like brake pad replacement develops into the expensive replacement of major brake components."

Want to know how to spend the minimum on your brakes and at the same time be certain that they are in the safest possible working order? Have a professional mechanic check the entire system out once a year. At that time, he or she will inspect all the working parts and tell you what percent of your brake pads and linings remain. The mechanic's estimate will depend to some extent on how you brake. We'll talk about braking habits that can save you money a little later.

Disc brakes have a convenient little peephole that allows a mechanic to look and see how much pad is left and how it's wearing. Drum brakes are in an enclosed system, so the mechanic will have to pull the drum off, which takes time and for which there's usually a charge. It's well worth the few dollars it costs to know how many miles these linings have left before they need to be replaced.

Front brakes wear faster than rear brakes, sometimes as much as twice as fast, so you can normally get away with having the front ones checked every year and the rear ones every other year. A good brake mechanic can practically tell by sitting in the car and feeling the pressure of the brake pedal how healthy or unhealthy the system is.

Check the brake fluid level in the master cylinder reservoir once a month, or have a professional check it for you. Most newer cars are equipped with translucent master cylinder reservoirs that allow you to check the fluid

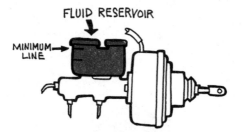

FLUID RESERVOIR

MINIMUM LINE

level without opening the container. On older models, however, the reservoir's top must be removed. Open the reservoir only after you have wiped it clean with a rag. Brake fluid hates dirt, and contaminated brake fluid has been responsible for more than one instance of brake failure. If you notice the fluid is disappearing on a regular basis, either your brake pads are wearing out or there is a leak in the system, perhaps in the master cylinder. In either case, regular fluid loss means something's up.

Avoid diagnosing brake problems yourself, unless you are a trained professional. Brake problems are not limited to what we have described here. Brake rotors and drums can warp or twist as a result of a number of different causes including the extreme heat of unusually hard braking or even incorrect tightening of the lug nuts. In addition, sounds can mean many things. Even a little dirt caught in the drum can cause a brake to make a grinding sound. Also, a drum that is simply not adjusted properly can result in an irregular or pulsating braking pattern. Get a second opinion before you have other than routine pad and lining replacement work done. As usual, call around for prices and get a complete list of what is included.

169

Brakes

The Parking Brake

On most cars, the parking or emergency brake works on the rear brakes. A system of cables extends from a knob, lever, or pedal located under the dashboard or on the floor

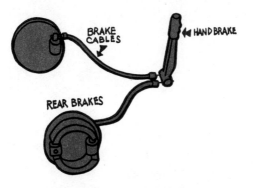

to the linings or pads of the rear brakes. When the parking brake is applied, the linings or pads are forced against the rear drums or rotors until released. Although it is designed to keep the car from moving after it has already stopped, it can be used to help stop the car if the regular brake system fails. If the parking brake is working correctly, the car should not move forward easily in Drive or first gear. With use, however, the cables stretch. Consequently, the pads or linings do not hold as snugly as they once did. Be sure your regular brake service includes a parking brake inspection and adjustment when necessary.

Antilock Brakes

Antilock systems have been around since the late 1940s but not on anything you might have driven unless you were a licensed commercial pilot. This add-on to the braking system helps prevent lock-up, which in an emergency breaking maneuver is most often responsible for the car going out of control.

First found on expensive heavy or high performance

cars and now increasingly available on standard passenger cars, antilock brakes help to provide better traction for the tires. While the types vary, the basic principle is that sensors or feelers are placed at each wheel or between two wheels that rotate together. An electronic control center (brain) receives messages about the behavior of each wheel in the form of voltage transmissions. If the car is in a hard braking maneuver, for example, an effort to avoid hitting a pedestrian who has stepped onto the road, the brakes may move with such force that the wheels lock up or freeze. If they do, traction is gone and the car slides uncontrollably.

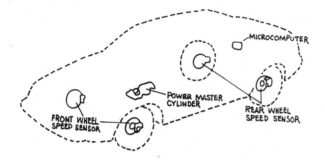

The control center senses that the brakes are about to lock and reduces fluid pressure to the brakes. The brakes maintain maximum braking action without allowing the wheels to lock up. This system actually provides the driver with a built-in expert braker for emergencies. If your budget can stand it, give this option careful consideration.

Making Your Brakes Last Longer

You may not know it, but you have a lot of control over how long your brake pads and linings will last by the way you apply the brake pedal. The way I see it, there are three different kinds of brakers. Braker A sees a stoplight three blocks away and continues at present speed until about 6 inches from the light, whereupon she slams on the brake, hurtling the unsuspecting passengers forward in their seats with a crisp neck-snapping motion. The wear generated by this type of braking action is major; the pads and linings get jammed against the rotors and/or drums because a lot of friction is needed to stop this car so

quickly. A lot of friction means a lot of heat and a lot of wear.

Braker B sees the same light three blocks away and gets off the accelerator, but now because Braker B really doesn't have anything else to do with it, that foot just rests lightly on the brake pedal—just a little, not so you'd notice, but enough to ensure that the brake pads and linings really heat up as they are constantly forced against the rotors and/or drums for the entire three blocks. This braking pattern causes the pads to wear excessively, and it also results in the formation of a glaze on the pads and/or linings, similar to the glass slipper effect that we talked about in chapter 8. Sometimes the glaze can be sanded off, but sometimes replacement is necessary. This braking pattern always costs the driver money in premature maintenance and repairs.

Braker C sees the same light three blocks away, but this driver, who knows the "Off-Off Rule," gets off the accelerator and lets the car coast slowly to a stop, touching the brake pedal only with a gentle but repetitious squeeze and release motion. The more moderate heat that is generated by this braking action is dissipated quickly as the brake pedal is released. These brakes will not only last many, many miles longer but will do a safer, more effective job. Good braking patterns and a yearly check of the entire braking system will go a long way to ensuring both peace of mind and smaller repair bills.

Tires and Other
Round Things

What would you say if I told you that the majority of cars on the road today are running on underinflated tires, that those underinflated tires can take up to 25 percent longer to stop your car, and that the loss of 25 percent in stopping power can be the margin of error you need to avoid being involved in an accident? Furthermore, underinflated tires get hotter; consequently, they are prone to blowouts. As if that weren't enough, underinflated tires cost you money, as they wear faster and deliver fewer miles to the gallon than properly inflated tires.

Despite the fact that it is typically overlooked in this self-serve world of ours, correct tire pressure plays a major role in your safety. In combination with your car's suspension, steering, and brake systems, traction (the tendency of a tire's rubber surface to stick to the road surface because of friction) is what keeps your car on the road and going in

TIRES

the direction you want, rather than the direction that the forces of nature, specifically, momentum, would like it to go.

Tires also provide a more pleasant ride, a nice pillow of air in the form of a spongy rubber shoe worn by your car's metal feet. The steel wheels are attached to the hubs located at the end of each axle by heavy metal bolts called lugs. The lugs are secured by lug nuts, the metal caps you will swear were glued on by a weightlifter if you ever have to remove them to change a tire. Unlike the wooden wagon wheels of pioneer times that endlessly jiggled and jostled their passenger's spines and dentures, tires isolate you from the jolting impact of the bumps, stones, potholes, and washboard surfaces over which you travel.

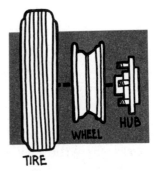

TIRE

Today's tires are constructed of a combination of fabrics and materials that are designed to provide a compromise between comfort, good road handling, and long wear.

In the early days, cars ran on skinny tires that looked like bicycle tires. These skinny tires were just a little overly responsive, and it was common to see cars in the ditch along the side of the road. A car was about as predictable as a skittish horse, and it would be a while before "steady as she goes" was a term that could be applied accurately to the automobile.

As cars grew larger and heavier and engine speeds increased, it was as if a tall, burly person was standing on skinny little feet. Consequently, cars needed greater stability in the form of a bigger, broader footprint, and the tire manufacturers responded. With wider tires available, the chances of a car's staying on the road improved dramatically. The chances improved even more with the addition of the grooves or channels cut in the smooth rubber of the tread (the part that comes in contact with the road).

But wait. If you read about sneakers in the chapters on the clutch and brakes, you remember that they generated friction when scuffed along a smooth surface, so you've probably guessed already that the best design for a tire would be a wide smooth one, with no grooves or indentations, one that would provide the maximum surface for contacting the road. If cuts or channels are made in this smooth surface, the amount of tire surface in direct contact with the road is reduced. But the grooves would provide drainage for water, mud, and snow, and sweep road surface deposits through and behind the tires so that secure contact with the road can be maintained. So which is it going to be—smooth or grooved tires? The answer is both.

Traction

It's true that perfectly smooth tires provide the best contact with the road. You will still see them on many race car tires where the least amount of resistance to forward speed is the key to success. The problem encountered in the use of grooveless tire treads is that when water, snow, sleet, mud, gravel, or any other deposits accumulate on the road surface, the tire loses contact with the road. Without contact, there is no friction; without friction, there is no traction; and without traction, the car cannot be controlled. Notice how quickly those drivers switch to rain tires (tires with grooves in them) or how quickly the race ends if it rains hard.

Unfortunately, unless you live in and never leave the Mohave Desert (any large desert will do), you can't always count on finding dry roads. A compromise that represents the best for both wet and dry conditions had to made. The construction of every modern tire is the direct result of the compromise between the conflicting needs of different road conditions and passenger comfort.

Bias-ply, Bias-belted, and Radial Tires

How well each tire meets these needs depends on the materials used in its construction, both inside and out, and their position in the tire. These materials are constantly changing, as tire manufacturers work toward improving their characteristics. There are three basic designs in tire construction: bias-ply, bias-belted, and radial. Usually the symbols indicating the materials of which the tire is made are stamped on the side of the tire. Knowing how to interpret that information can help you choose a quality product and correct replacement tire for your car.

The construction of a tire begins with its "bead," thin strips of metal wound together into a narrow ring that provides an airtight grip on the wheels. Attached to the bead are pieces of material called "plies." Plies were originally made of cotton, but later much stronger fabrics such as nylon, polyester, and other synthetics, as well as steel, replaced cotton. It is the material of the ply and the angle at which the threads or cords of the plies meet each other that determines the construction category into which the tire falls.

Bias-ply and bias-belted plies both meet each other on the diagonal, at an angle of roughly 35 to 40 degrees. The principal difference between the two is that bias-belted tires have strips of metal or fiberglass incorporated within them which make the tires stiffer, improve their cornering capability, and extend their useful life. Radial tires have plies that meet each other at right angles, that is, 90 degrees. The smaller the angle, the better the road handling capability. The larger the angle, the cushier the ride.

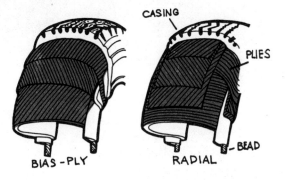

With such a large angle, you might think that radials would deliver a very smooth ride, but what about performance? Their sides move when cornering, which should make their road-gripping qualities unacceptable, except that like the bias-belted tires, radials get their performance characteristics from the strips of steel added between the plies and the tread, strips that in turn increase stability and extend tire life.

Radial tires, with which most newer cars are equipped, while providing excellent cornering characteristics as their sides flex to keep the whole of the tire on the ground, can generate more noise and a rougher ride at lower speeds. Combining the best road handling with the most comfortable ride is the aim of every tire. Some do it better than others, but there is always a compromise.

Tire Ratings

Now you're ready to read the symbols on the side of the tire. The first set of symbols you'll see relates to the size and general type of tire construction. P stands for passenger vehicle. The next numbers you see, for example, 180, represent the width of the tire measured in millimeters. The number 55 is a ratio that represents the proportion of the tire's height to its width; the tire's height is 55 percent of its width. The letter R indicates the way in which the tire is constructed. R is for radial, D means bias-ply, and B is for bias-belted. The number 13 indicates the diameter of the wheel (not the tire) as measured in inches.

Tire quality is rated according to three categories: traction, resistance to heat, and mileage. The word "Traction" on the tire followed by a letter grade of A to C, with C being the lowest measure, indicates the relative capability of the tire to stop on a wet road surface. The resistance of the tire to heat—how hot or cool it runs long distance at highway speeds—is indicated by the word "Temperature" followed by a letter grade of A to C, where again C is the lowest measure. How many miles you can expect to get out of a tire is indicated by the word "Treadware" followed by a number from 50 to 350, which represents the potential average tire wear for that tire. In addition to these ratings, however, it is important to remember that tire wear is also to a large extent determined by how you drive (high speed driving causes more heat and thus more wear), where you drive (substandard roads take their toll on rubber), and tire maintenance (inflation).

As with most other items you buy, the quality of the tires will be reflected to some degree by the price you pay, but remember that the best quality tires go on sale and that you're in a good position to take advantage of getting the most for your money by not waiting until you need an immediate replacement. When you're buying tires, investigate thoroughly before paying for the most expensive. Be sure to get those with the qualities that reflect your individual driving needs. In other words, if you drive mostly on paved highways at highway speeds (the legal ones) and you buy an extremely high performance tire, you may be paying for tire qualities that you do not need.

All-season versus Mud/Snow Tires

The tread on a snow tire has especially deep grooves, which are specifically designed to claw away at the snow and ice in order to dig down and make contact with the road surface below. This aggressive tread works great on ice and snow, but it wears faster on dry roads than a conventional tread does. All-season tires last longer than snow tires and still do a reasonably good job of handling bad weather road conditions. If you live in an area where the average snow and ice accumulation is marginal, all-season tires can save you some money by limiting you to one set of tires. No matter how good the all-season tire is, however, if you live in an area where winters are harsh and ice or snow storms are common, snow tires are a wise investment.

CONVENTIONAL   MUD/SNOW   STUDDED   CHAINS

Studded tires, while not legal in all states, offer even more traction in the toughest of conditions. Chains may also be an option if you live in an area where you get heavy snow but only occasionally. Although they're easier to install than they were years ago, putting chains on still means getting out of the car in the snow and crawling around on your hands and knees.

Regardless of the type or quality of tire you choose, your tires need your help to perform properly. For many years when full-service gas stations were the rule, not the more expensive exception, that help came from a service attendant who would, when asked, check the pressure in your tires. It was not uncommon for an attendant to even point out that a tire looked low or that a tread was badly worn. It was a reassuring feeling to think that someone else was occasionally concerned about the health of your car.

Not so today. Even when you are willing to pay the substantially higher price per gallon to patronize a full-service station, the attendants do not, as a rule, check air pressure. Consequently, you are increasingly "on your own" in providing for this vital maintenance check. If you overlook it, you are jeopardizing your own safety. Luckily, checking tire pressure and the general health of your tires is as simple as brushing your teeth.

When a tire has too much air pressure (is overinflated), only its stomach touches the road surface. The tire's shoulders are pulled up and away from the road. A little bit of stomach tread is all that is making contact with the road. The number of grooves able to push water and snow away is reduced. It's like having a skinnier tire on the car. The tread wear pattern, which you may or may not see (it is less visible with radial tires), indicates lots of tread left on the shoulders (why should they wear when they're not touching the road?) and little tread left on the stomach, which is getting all the wear.

When a tire does not have enough air pressure (is underinflated), its shoulders sag and puff out, and its stomach treads are pulled up and in away from the pavement. A little bit of shoulder tread is all that is making

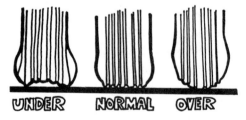

UNDER   NORMAL   OVER

contact with the road. In the case of an overinflated tire, the efficiency of the grooves that push water and snow away is reduced. You may feel the car pull to the right or left, or hear a squealing sound from the tires only when they corner, or you may see a tread wear pattern that is uneven, with lots of tread left in the middle (why should they wear when they're not touching the road?) and little tread left on the outside.

If overinflated tires have too much air and under-inflated tires too little, then properly inflated tires must have just the right amount of air—and so they do. A properly inflated tire has just enough air pressure in it to ensure that the maximum amount of tread (both shoulders and stomach) makes contact with the road. With all available rubber doing its job, the greatest traction is now possible. The nice part is that checking tire pressure is easy, inexpensive, and it makes a major contribution to your safety. Who could ask for anything more?

To check tire pressure, first buy yourself a good quality tire gauge. Buy the middle or top of the line gauge in any retail or auto parts store. They're generally more accurate and will last longer than the cheapest. Tire gauges come in two basic types: pencil and dial. Both work fine. Just be sure the one you buy can measure inflation up to 55 pounds since the smaller spare tires usually need this higher pressure, and you want to be able to check the pressure in the spare as well.

To find the correct pressure for your car's tires, should you use the convenient numbers stamped on the side of the tire? If you said no, you get a gold star. The numbers that are stamped on the side of the tire tell you the maximum tire pressure for that tire, not the specific manufacturer's recommendation for your particular car. The numbers that should interest you are found on a metal tag located in the glove compartment or inside one of the front door jambs. (On newer cars, the inclusion of this information is a law.) If all else fails, try your owner's manual, and if you are still without success, call a local dealership or tire store. Don't be shy about asking—this is your safety we're talking about. But whatever you do, don't assume that the air pressure in your tires is correct because they look okay. They need to be checked, all of them, and regularly.

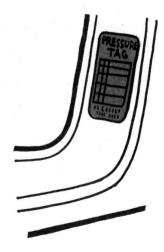

When you find the tag on the jamb or in the glove box it will say "Cold Tire Pressure" followed by many numbers. It's best to check air pressure in the morning if possible, before driving the car more than a mile or two. Heat causes the air inside the tires to expand. If driven more than a few miles, or if it is an exceptionally hot day, the tires will give a false reading that will indicate there is more pressure in the tire than there actually is. The letter F stands for front tire pressure and letter R stands for rear tire pressure. These numbers may be the same or they may be different.

Now you are ready to check the pressure. Begin by locating the valve stem, the small plastic tube that sticks out of the side of the tire. You will not need to remove the wheel cover or hub cap unless the cover hides the valve stem or makes it inaccessible. (If the valve stems on your tires are hard to reach, ask at an auto parts store if a valve stem extender is available. Extenders screw onto the original valve stem, lengthening it and making it easier to reach.) Remove the protective cap on the valve stem. If you're using a pencil-type gauge, be sure that you push the nylon tab (with the numbers along it) all the way in before you start. Apply the gauge to the valve stem at a right angle and push firmly; the tiny pin inside the gauge should meet the pin inside the valve stem. You will hear a whoosh of air, which is normal. No, you are not letting all the air out of your tires. (That is, of course, unless you continue to push on the pin, in which case you will let all the air out.) The firmer and more directly you apply the gauge, the less air will leak out. The nylon tab will pop out of the bottom of the gauge, revealing a number. If you're using a dial type, the needle will move from zero to a number. In either case, the number will indicate the amount of air pressure in pounds per inch.

TIRE VALVE

If the number on the dial isn't the same as the number on the metal tag, it means the amount of air is either too high or too low. Neither one will do. Let's take the low pressure first. You checked the pressure as directed and found the front two tires are down 3 pounds. Now endure the real insult to the modern-day consumer and prepare to pay for the air you will need to add, in other words, those 3 pounds. If it's free, you're lucky. Drive to a service station, hopefully one not more than a few miles away. Test the pressure again while at the station to determine if it has risen in the few minutes it took to make the trip. Note the difference. If it is farther than a few miles or the weather is particularly hot, remember the reading from home or wherever you originally checked it and add only as much as indicated by your original test.

If the station's air tower gauge is accurate, it's unusual. That's why you have your own gauge. If you get carried away and put too much air in, use the small tip or pin on the back of the tire gauge and push it against the valve stem to release some air. Then test the pressure again. If it is the first time you've ever done this, you may want to bring your lunch.

Checking tire pressure every time you check the oil makes good sense. And remembering to examine the spare once a month is an important part of the job. Even though spares are just sitting around, they do lose air. You'd be plenty upset if you ever needed it and the darn thing was flat as a pancake. Always check tire pressure before going on a trip, long or short. Long trips heat up tires normally; if the tires are also underinflated, you could be unknowingly asking for a blowout.

Improper tire inflation also contributes to a scary driving condition known as hydroplaning. Have you ever been driving along on a wet road and all of a sudden you get this weird feeling—à la Twilight Zone—that your car is floating? It may be. If your car is hydroplaning, floating is exactly what it's doing. Tire grooves can push only so much water through them before they fill. When this happens, a layer of water is formed between the tire and the road surface. As the car rides up on the water, it is temporarily disconnected from the road surface. Traction and

WATER

control go right out the window. Slowing your car's speed helps regain traction by allowing the grooves more time to work, but in the meantime you are in no-man's-land. The possibility of hydroplaning is dramatically decreased if the tire treads are in good shape, if the tire pressure is correct, and you don't drive 180 mph through large puddles.

What about those little spares? Small or "doughnut" spare tires are good at doing what they're designed for, which is to save storage space. At a speed no greater than that stamped on the side of the tire, they are designed to get you to a service station so that you can have the original tire fixed. Trouble may result if they are pushed beyond their design capabilities. They are not intended to serve as a fifth tire, as a full-size spare, that is, to be run at highway speeds and to be replaced when and if it's convenient. As an added bonus, you don't have to be Mountain Man Dean to get it out of the trunk if you do have to change a flat tire.

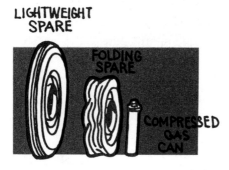

When I first started presenting car care workshops, I traveled throughout New England, mostly by car. I was frequently on the road late at night, in bad weather, and in areas where I really did not want to be stranded. The presence of a full-sized tire (despite the fact that it took up a lot of storage space and made getting my full-sized, four-cylinder engine demonstrator in the back of my car a job for a contortionist) and the knowledge that I knew how to change it safely with my eyes closed, gave me the extra peace of mind that I needed. (More about changing tires at the end of this chapter.)

If you really hate the small-size spares, consider buying another full-sized wheel and tire and put it in the back of your car. It may be well worth the exchange in storage space that you sacrifice for the peace of mind it may bring.

If you buy a wheel and full-sized tire to replace your small spare, you'll generally find it cheaper to buy from a secondhand lot. Be sure, however, that you look carefully at the tread for signs of unevenness and irregular wear, and check the rim of the wheel carefully for heavy rust, dents, or irregularities. Much of the equipment in secondhand lots has been taken off wrecks. It's easy to get stuck with a wheel that's not round or a tire that's already had significant tread wear, neither of which will work adequately if you need to use it.

It's not necessary to wait until the tire's steel belts that attach it to the wheel are exposed and whipping gaily around as you drive down the road or your tires fail a state inspection to replace them. There are a number of ways to evaluate the condition of your tires. Even if you are not a tire expert, you can observe and determine their condition with an inexpensive tread depth indicator, or cheaper still, a penny.

When inserted into various grooves in the tire, the indicator will show a number. If the number is less than 1/16 inch, it's time to begin looking for a replacement. If you're using a penny, insert it into various grooves and find Lincoln's forehead. If it's visible, think about replacing the tire. It doesn't mean you have to race to the nearest retail store and buy the most expensive tires available; it does mean you should begin seriously comparing tire quality and prices and replace the tires within a reasonable time.

Today's tires also have wear bar indicators in them. A wear bar is a patch of smooth rubber inserted into the tread of the tire. As the tire wears to about a 1/16 inch depth, these smooth patches of rubber appear in what otherwise looks like a normal tread. They will always be seen across two or more treads. They are a warning that there is still decent tread left, but you should begin the process of looking for replacement tires now.

Tire Rotation

When you stop, all the weight in the car shifts forward. In addition, the front wheels steer, and if your car is front wheel drive, the front wheels drive. It is no wonder the front tires wear faster than the rear ones (on front wheel drive cars, the front tires may wear twice as fast as the rear tires). Most tires should be rotated on a regular basis to equalize the uneven front tire wear with the slower paced wear of the rear tires. In effect, rotation distributes that uneven wear. Instead of replacing the front tires as they wear, you can rotate them to the back where the wear pattern will be evened out. Switching tires in this way can give you the most life out of a set of tires. In addition, you will have the treads of both sets of tires in a healthier state, not one set in good shape and one worn.

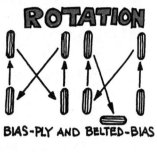

BIAS-PLY AND BELTED-BIAS

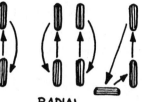

RADIAL

What method should I use to rotate my tires? Your owner's manual should tell you not only how to rotate tires but whether you should. Some manufacturers do not recommend rotation. If your owner's manual doesn't say, take the advice of a qualified mechanic, dealer, or reputable tire replacement store. Bias-ply and bias-belted tires are rotated in a crisscross pattern, while radials are rotated front to back with the tires staying on the same side of the car. Again, the configuration in your owner's manual is the one you should follow.

If you switch to snow tires or any other alternative set of tires during the year, make sure the tires are marked as they are removed from the car. Their position on the car should be written on the tire with chalk or some other easily readable, nonpermanent marker.

Alignment

Should you have your car aligned? Absolutely. Alignment has to do with the angle, made by the suspension components, at which the car's wheels meet the road. It's a compromise angle, because to get the most out of their treads, your tires would like to roll soldier-straight down the road. This position would maximize their useful lives. But a soldier-straight relationship to the road does not promote

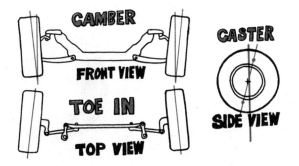

CAMBER
FRONT VIEW
TOE IN
TOP VIEW

CASTER
SIDE VIEW

good road handling. The car would feel heavy and unresponsive as it went through turns. You'd feel as if you were driving a Mack truck. For the car to handle well, the tires need to sit slightly off the vertical, slightly tilted to the road surface. Wheel alignment creates an angle that best accommodates both of these needs.

Several different measurements are taken and corrected according to the manufacturer's suggestions in an alignment procedure; the most common are caster, camber, toe-in, and toeout. Without proper alignment, you may feel the car drift in either direction, you may hear a squealing sound coming from wheels all the time, or you may see an irregular tread wear pattern on the tire with wear accelerated on one side only. The bottom line is the tires will wear faster.

If you want to get the most out of a set of tires, have an alignment done at least once a year. The frequency of alignment depends on the type of driving you do and the road conditions. If the road surface over which you drive is full of great potholes that jar your teeth and limbs as you drop into them, if you're fond of gravity force starts and quarterhorse stops, if you park on the curb instead of next to it, your need for more frequent alignment increases proportionately.

Wheel Balancing

What about wheel balancing? It's a must. The trouble with wheels is they're not round. Oh, they think they're round, and they even look round, but they're not. They have heavier spots on them that cause them to turn irregularly rather than in a nice smooth circle. You may feel this imbalance as a vibration when you drive, or you may see the results in the form of an irregular tread wear pattern called cupping or scalloping. Along the same groove you'll see healthy tread, worn tread, healthy tread, and so on.

To compensate for a tire's unevenness, small pieces of metal, called weights, are attached to the lighter spots on the wheels to balance out the heavy spots and to make the wheel turn evenly. There are a couple of popular ways to balance tires: static and dynamic. A static balancing takes place with the wheel off the car. It doesn't allow for the influence of the brakes and suspension components as well as a dynamic balancing, which is done on the car.

Tires should be balanced each time they come off the rim. If you remove a tire simply to look at something else, the weights remain untouched. Over time, the weights can fall off and the balancing will have to be done again, even if the tire did not come off the rim. An unbalanced wheel can eventually damage the wheel bearings (see chap. 9 for more on wheel bearings). It's best not to wait until damage is done.

Dealing with the Dreaded Flat Tire

You're driving down the road, it's late, it's night, and you hear a loud pop. The car swerves violently. You get off the accelerator and with firm, steady, but unlocked, arms you pick a safe spot on the side of the road and ease the car over to it. The first thing you do upon landing is put the emergency flashers on and set the parking brake with the car turned off and in park or first gear.

After exiting the car by the door away from the road, you pull out your fully equipped emergency kit. In it is a good flashlight with batteries that work! You take the piece of fluorescent material—vest, ribbon, anything you can drape over your body—and put it on so you show up in the dark. (Flat tires only happen when you're in your best black and pearls or in a dark colored suit.) Now take one of the two flares from the emergency kit, which you have wrapped tightly in plastic to prevent moisture from destroying them.

You walk backward 6 to 10 car lengths and light the first of the 2 flares as you would a big match. First take the top plastic cover off. You'll find a striking surface underneath. Now remove the second, larger plastic cover under which you will find another striking surface. Hold the flare away from your face and briskly rub striking surface against striking surface. The flare may spit sparks at you, so keep it away from your clothing as you stick it in the ground or lay it on its side. Most flares will burn for only 15 minutes. That's why you have two.

Return to the car and remove your owner's manual from the glove box where you stashed it on that beautiful day last spring, after having carefully read the instructions for the use of your jack, and just before you practiced the following procedure in the warmth and comfort of your own well-lighted driveway or garage with several of your closest friends for company.

You are now armed and ready to calmly get yourself back on the road. You remove from their appointed storage spots all the required paraphernalia: jack, standard equipment lug wrench, special 4-way (star lug wrench, which you also purchased that day last spring at a local auto parts or retail store), spare tire, plastic chock (block), and optional garden gloves.

You place the chock behind the opposite wheel of the one that is flat. This is to ensure that even if the car did slip off the jack, the car wouldn't roll. Remove the wheel covering using the method and device shown in your manual; keep it handy. Now position the jack as your manual indicates, but do not raise the car with it yet. First you'll have to break the tension on the lug nuts. Since they have undoubtedly been put on with an air tool, which has the strength of eight giant men, and since you probably don't lift weights for a living, you will need to use the star wrench to increase your leverage. Take the wrench, which has been purchased specifically for your car. You had two choices when you bought yours: one is for domestic (SAE) and one is for foreign (metric). If you have chosen correctly, one of the ends of the wrench—you may have to try them all—will fit snugly onto the lug nuts.

Right is Tight. Right is Tight. Right is Tight. Unless the lug nut says "L." If the lug nuts on your wheel say nothing, you can assume that the direction in which they must be turned to remove them is to the left, or counterclockwise. If they say "L," you will need to remove them in the opposite direction. But you already know which way they go because you practiced last spring. Remember?

Stand slightly toward the front of the tire, and as you pull one of the arms of the lug wrench toward you, push your foot down on the other end. Keep your hips underneath you. It is the weight of your lower body that you are trying to use here. Break the tension on each of the lug nuts in this way, but don't remove them. Now slowly engage the jack, standing again slightly to one side in case it decides to snap at your ankles. Raise the car only as high as is necessary to remove the old tire and put the new one on. You can always raise it another notch if it's too short, but the higher it goes, the less stable it is.

Now remove the lug nuts the rest of the way by hand and put then inside the hub cap. If you miss this step and you accidentally kick one in the dirt, you can bet finding it in the dark will be less than rewarding. Take the old tire off, being particularly careful not to touch the rubber until you're sure it's cool. Blowouts pump temperatures inside tires to tropical levels, and they may remain hot for quite a while. This is where those garden gloves look better and better. Put the spare on. Take the lug nuts and hand tighten them in a crisscross pattern until as you're tightening them each one starts to make the wheel spin. Then go back and check each one again. Slowly lower the jack. Take that star lug wrench and crank each one of those lugs

with all your might. Right is Tight. Unless you are here
from another planet and have superhuman strength, you
can't overtighten lugs with your hands. Stow the rest of
the goodies back where they came from and drive to a service station and have the original tire repaired. If the
spare is a full-sized spare that can be rotated into your
regular tires and is designed for doing so, you can continue
to drive on it, but have the tension on the lug nuts checked
by a professional.

If you, for whatever reason, do not feel comfortable
with any or all of the above procedure, use Plan B: take the
fluorescent sign that is also in your emergency kit—the
one that says HELP PLEASE CALL THE POLICE—and
place it in the rear window so that the traffic going in your
direction can easily see it, lock your door, and only open it
for a uniformed policeman or legitimate tow truck
representative. If someone else stops to help you, the safest
thing you can do under most circumstances is to thank
them for their offer of help through a window open only
enough for them to hear your request for a police officer
and tow truck. It doesn't take a very wide opening to do
that.

Bear in mind that there is no one set of correct rules
for appropriately dealing with every emergency situation.
Your response will have to be conditioned by your knowledge of the area, the weather, the general safety of the
road, and many other variables. As in any emergency situation, you will need to use your common sense. There is
only one rule that always applies: your safety and that of
your passengers comes first. Whatever it takes.

There may be a situation in which you're stuck on a
narrow bridge or in a tunnel and there is no safe place to
pull off the road; in that case, you will have to continue to
drive the car **at a reduced speed** with the emergency
flashers until you reach a safe spot to exit the road. That
means the wheel will probably get smooshed and the tire
shredded—a small price to pay for your safety.

If you car is parked somewhere and you return to find
a slow leak has taken its invisible hissing toll, a can of tire
sealant is a good way to avoid having to change a tire. It
will get your car, driven slowly, to a nearby service station

to have the tire repaired. Sealant usually doesn't work for a blowout because there's rarely enough rubber left to seal. If you do use sealant, read the instructions on the label, and be sure you notify the mechanic that you have used it. It needs to be cleaned out and removed immediately.

Choosing and Dealing with a Mechanic

Wouldn't it be wonderful if every time your car broke down a fairy god-mechanic appeared and, with a wave of her magic ratchet, turned your lemon into a dream car? Unfortunately, mechanics in the real world are of the mere mortal variety. If you own a car, sooner or later you are going to have to pick one to work on it.

Choosing a mechanic is a task most consumers approach with all the fear, loathing, and paranoia they can muster. It doesn't have to be that way. The mechanics of this world are not all out to get us. But just as in any other profession, their ranks include the good, the bad, and the indifferent.

To be sure, there are a great many incompetent and unskilled mechanics. In most states, all those with a rusty screwdriver and the inclination can call themselves mechanics and offer to operate on your car. For the few states that do require certification or licensing of mechanics, the requirements to qualify are usually very minimal. As cars become more sophisticated, the situation worsens.

The problem of incompetence is worsened by the shortage of people entering the field and the large number who are leaving. To complicate matters further, there are some in the field who, although they are skilled, lack scruples. The widespread incompetence and dishonesty in the field has been demonstrated over the last ten years in both public and private studies. The results show there is less than a 50 percent chance of getting a repair job done correctly and for a reasonable price on the first try.

Nevertheless, there are still a lot of mechanics who are skilled and honest, and it is possible for you to find one. You don't even need a degree in auto repair, just common sense and the willingness to do some detective work.

Word of Mouth

When stalking a good mechanic, word of mouth is probably the best method. Ask your friends, relatives, and co-workers where or to whom they take their autos for servicing. Finding a qualified and honest mechanic can be just that easy.

Use your common sense before acting on their recommendations. Just because Uncle Joe tells you he got a real good deal from SeeU-Soon Auto Repair when they changed the oil in his car, it doesn't mean you should rush right down there and have your ailing transmission fixed. Even though the mechanics at See-U-Soon may be wizards at changing oil, it could be that they wouldn't know a transmission if it crashed through the roof and landed with a bang in the garage bay.

It's prudent to be wary. Ask questions. What kind of work was done on Uncle Joe's car? Did the shop do just the work requested or did they make additional repairs? Did they exceed the estimate? If so, was there a valid reason, and was Joe notified first? Is Uncle Joe known for his good judgment, or does he own 50 acres of swampland in Florida? These are some of the questions that will get you the answers you need to make an intelligent decision.

Don't make the common mistake of restricting your choice to those shops closest to your home. A garage within walking distance is a great convenience, but should your car break down because Near-Your-House Service Shop didn't do the job right, you could find yourself a long, long way from home.

If your car is under warranty, you'll have to use an approved repair shop or authorized dealership. This doesn't mean that you haven't any options. First, you may still have a choice of the approved shops in your area. Second, you may be able to choose which one of a particular shop's mechanics will work on your car. And third, even if your options are limited, you can still learn how best to deal with that shop or mechanic to ensure that your needs are met.

Other Methods

Although personal referral is one of the best ways to find a good mechanic, it is not the only way. There are other sources of this information. Automobile clubs, in addition to providing emergency road service, are also knowledgeable about good repair shops in your area. The American Automobile Association (AAA) is one of the largest and best known of these clubs. Their "Approved Auto Repair Program" has identified more than 4,000 auto repair facilities in 26 states that meet AAA standards of consistent, high-quality repair work and service. Consult your yellow pages. Shops with auto club approval usually mention that fact in their ads. Or call the auto clubs in your area for information.

The National Institute for Auto Service Excellence (NIASE) certifies mechanics through a series of eight written multiple choice tests, each covering a different system of the car. NIASE was created by the automotive industry; therefore, its objectivity and usefulness to the consumer should be evaluated within that context. Moreover, a passing score on a multiple-choice test is not a guarantee of competence in hands-on automotive repair, and it says nothing about a mechanic's ethics. Still, NIASE certification is probably better than nothing at all. Although NIASE does not provide a list of its certified mechanics, repair shops employing them usually display signs to that effect. Some of a shop's mechanics may not be certified or may not be certified in all eight categories. Make sure the one who works on your car is certified for that particular repair area.

Before you take your car into a new shop, don't forget to call the Consumer Complaint Division of your Attorney General's Office or the Better Business Bureau in your area. They won't recommend a mechanic or a shop, but they will tell you if the one you're considering has unresolved complaints filed against it.

Don't Wait

It's best not to wait until you are in the vulnerable position of needing major repair work to try out a new shop or mechanic. Bring the car in first for a minor repair or routine maintenance job, such as an oil change or tire rotation.

On that first visit, give the garage area the "once over." Is it reasonably organized and clean? Or does it look like it's been stirred with a large spoon? Does it have computerized diagnostic tools? Or is the mechanic equipped with a large wrench, rusty screwdriver, and little else?

Today's new cars require sophisticated equipment to make certain types of repairs and tune-ups. "Black boxes," which run computerized ignitions, and fuel injectors have replaced mechanical parts such as carburetors and points. You need to know whether this mechanic has the manuals and instruments needed to work on the computerized systems of your car. Some of the smaller shops do great work even though they can't afford the computerized machines necessary for more technical repairs and adjustments. Are they honest enough to tell you what they can't do? And if they can't do a job, can they refer you to another reputable shop for the type of work you require?

The most important consideration in choosing a mechanic is not equipment but attitude. Initial encounters should leave you feeling comfortable with the way you were treated. If you and your mechanic cannot establish a rapport on repairs, chances are the relationship won't last for long. A long-term association with a single repair shop or mechanic is the best way for them to get to know you and your car.

If you're still waiting for the fairy god-mechanic to appear, forget it. Start looking for the next best thing—a fair and good mechanic. You could turn your grim tales of automotive woe into stories that end happily with you driving off into the sunset.

Specialists versus General Practitioners

Just as the medical world is full of specialists—doctors who only work on hearts, or ears, or feet—so, too, is the automotive world. There are shops that work only on engines or that only do transmission work. Other common specialties are front end work, mufflers and exhaust, body work, tires and suspension, brakes, 15-minute oil changes, and one-hour tune-ups. Is it better to deal with a specialist or a general practitioner when it comes to your car? The answer depends on your priorities.

Many of the specialists promise to save you time and money, and many do just that while also providing quality work. Nevertheless, when you use a specialist for a particular car problem, you are missing an opportunity to establish or continue a relationship with a single shop or mechanic—a general practitioner. By taking all your routine maintenance and repairs to one place, your mechanic gets to know you and your car better.

A specialty shop may save you time and money. But a routine oil change and lube is a good way for you to test the work of a new mechanic at a nonspecialty shop. A major repair is not a job you want to take to a stranger.

When it comes to certain items, such as tires, a specialist may be less expensive than an independent shop or the dealership. High volume usually allows the specialist to charge less and still make a profit. Call each and compare their prices. Always be sure that the prices you are comparing are for items of the same quality. If the specialty shop is using parts of inferior quality, those big savings in time and money may not be much of a bargain.

Quality workmanship, as well as parts, is a major consideration when choosing between a specialist and a generalist. Are the people who work on your car qualified and well trained, or did they just do their first lube job this morning? And finally, are parts and labor guaranteed? Specialty shops are usually less expensive, but there may be trade-offs for those savings.

Diagnostic Centers

New on the automotive repair scene are diagnostic centers, which can give you a complete or partial checkup of your car's systems and an assessment of its condition. Such centers are very useful if you're seeking a first or second opinion before taking your car in for maintenance or repair. The problem is that many of these centers are linked to repair shops and may exist to drum up business for them. They could try to con you into unneeded repairs. Your best bet is to choose a diagnostic center that is not associated with any repair shop (they are rare, but they do exist), or make it very clear that if problems are found you intend to take the car to a shop that is not associated with the diagnostic center. This takes courage, but you can do it.

Dealing with a Mechanic

Describing Symptoms

Finding a good mechanic is essential, but it is not enough to ensure good car care. Just as mechanics are not fairy godmothers, they are also not magicians or psychics or even private detectives. Before your mechanic can diagnose or fix the problem, he or she needs to know what symptoms have brought you and your car to the garage.

The Five Senses

The use of the five senses—hearing, sight, smell, taste, and touch—is the key to explaining your car's troubles to the mechanic and getting them solved.

Hearing: Noise is one of the more common ways your car will let you know it is not happy. Cries, sobs, whimpers, screams, moans, grumbling, cussing—yes, cars in pain do complain but in their own language. Any of these sounds (or others your car may create) could mean your car is heading for a breakdown or a repair. (Or it could mean you just ran over Fluffy the Cat. If it's Fluffy, the sound will probably go away.) If the sound persists, you need to get the car checked. Isolate the sound. Is it coming from the front, rear, left, right, under the hood, inside the dash, in a wheel well, from the engine?

The vocabulary of your ailing car:

Sight: Is your dashboard trying to tell you something? Are the warning lights on or flickering? Is the needle of any gauge out of its normal range? If so, you may have a problem with your battery, alternator, brakes, engine temperature, or oil pressure. Watch for the visual signs of a problem such as a leak, smoke, and steam. To make sure the spot on the pavement is yours and not from the car that parked there earlier, slide a piece of cardboard under the car and check it after a reasonable period. Note the source of the leak—front, rear, middle, left, right, engine. What color is it—gray, blue, black, white? Where is it coming from—tail pipe, under the car, from the engine compartment, a nearby garage shelf?

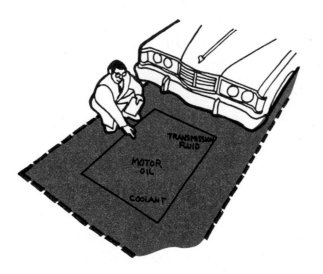

Smell: Cars can be quite odorous especially when they are trying to get your attention. If you have a leak, you might want to touch your finger to the spot on the ground and sniff the fluid. Most people can recognize the smell of gasoline. Coolant smells sweet. If your car smokes or steams, or even if there are no visual signals, it could be giving off a particular smell. Does it smell like rotten eggs, or burning rubber, metal, or toast?

Taste: If you have licked, nibbled, or eaten any part of your car for any reason, you probably need more help than a mechanic will be able to give you. Don't taste anything or let any fluid touch an open sore or cut.

Touch: Your car may exhibit symptoms of ill health in the way it handles or "feels" to you. Does it pull to the left or the right? Does the car vibrate, shimmy, shake, sputter, surge, hesitate, stall, or continue running after you turn off the ignition? Is the car hard to steer or does the steering feel loose or sloppy? When you press the brake pedal

does it feel spongy or too hard? Or does the pedal slowly
sink to the floor after you've stopped?

The Three Cs: Changes, Conditions, and Communications

Changes: Remember the three Cs when explaining the
symptoms to your mechanic. Change is often the first sign
of a car problem. Has your car suddenly or gradually
become different in the way it handles or sounds? Does it
drink more fluids lately such as oil, coolant, transmission
or brake fluid? Is it thirstier at the gas pump? If it has a
rattle in the rear end that sounds like Uncle Harry got
locked in the trunk, but the car has had that noise since
you bought it three years ago, you might not want to
worry about it. But if the rattle just started an hour ago
and it's getting worse by the minute, then you will probably want to have it checked. At least check the trunk. It
could be a loose jack, or it really might be Uncle Harry.

Conditions: Under what conditions does the particular
symptom occur? In first gear? In reverse? Between 40 and
50 mph? When you turn to the left? To the right? Uphill?
Downhill? When you're braking? Coasting? Accelerating?
Stopped? When you first start the car or after it has
warmed up? When it's raining? When it's cold? When the
heater is on? Only when you run over Fluffy? Is the symptom always there? Or does it come and go for no apparent
reason?

Communications: After you've figured out as much as
you can about what, how, when, and where your car's
annoying symptom occurs, you must accurately communicate that information to your mechanic. Don't trust these
details to memory—yours or your mechanic's. Write everything down. Even if you explain your problem to your

mechanic, it's still a good idea to write it down as well. If you take your car to a large repair shop with legions of mechanics, you might also want to tape a copy of the symptoms to the steering wheel. The mechanic you talk to may not be the one who works on your car. Whenever possible (it can never hurt to ask), talk to the person who will actually be working on your car.

Below is an example of what you need to give your mechanic before anyone begins working on your car. Note these essential elements: (1) symptoms—as defined by the five senses and the three Cs above; (2) a telephone number where you can be reached; and (3) request for an estimate. The most technical term in this letter is "tail pipe," proof you don't need to study mechanical engineering to communicate satisfactorily to your mechanic.

Dear Mechanic:
When I'm driving uphill at about 40 miles per hour, a whining sound comes from under the hood of my car which sounds like a big mosquito, then the car immediately stalls. It only does this on warm days (temperature above 75 degrees) and only after the car has been running for at least 15 minutes. After waiting at least a half hour, I am able to restart the car, at which time a big cloud of black smoke blows out of the tail pipe. Please call me at 555-1111 after your diagnosis to let me know how much you estimate the work will cost, if it is to be in excess of $50. Thank you.
Sincerely,
Hope Itzminor

The second and last thing to remember about communications is: Describe—don't diagnose. If you developed a stomachache, you wouldn't ask your doctor to remove your appendix, would you? No-oo-o. You'd say you had a pain in your abdomen and maybe that you were running a fever. The doctor would decide on the remedy.

The same is true of cars and mechanics. If your car stalls and your neighbor tells you she had the exact same problem last month and the mechanic had to replace her car's carburetor, that doesn't mean you should walk into your service station and ask your mechanic to replace the carburetor. Your car might only need a minor adjustment. Tell the mechanic what your car is doing. Describe the symptoms and let the mechanic make the diagnosis.

Maintenance Log

Make yourself a maintenance log out of a spiral-bound notebook small enough to fit in the glove compartment, or buy one in a store for a few dollars and change it to fit your needs. Record everything that happens to your car, for example, when you add fluids, oil, coolant, brake fluid, power steering fluid, and how much. Just noting that oil was added isn't specific enough for you to track accurately: ¼ or ½ quart of what weight oil is what you want to record along with the mileage and the date. Mark down which belts are changed, what filters are replaced, and any repairs that are made.

In the same notebook, keep track of your mileage. It's like keeping your finger on your car's pulse. A decrease in mileage over a short period of time is a sign that all is not

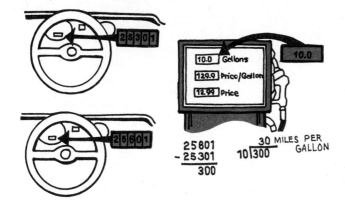

well and signals internal changes that may require simple adjustments or repairs to bring them back to normal. You are in a far more powerful position to help the technician diagnose a problem if you've been keeping accurate records. Keeping records may seem like a pain in the neck at first, but after a while it'll be like brushing your teeth, a habit so ingrained that you would be uncomfortable not doing it.

Get a written estimate. You've probably heard this advice over and over again when it comes to car repairs. In fact, many states have laws that require written estimates at least for more expensive repairs. Other laws may also require shops to get your consent to exceed the estimate, return replaced parts (with certain exceptions), provide written invoices itemizing parts and labor, and more. Check with the Attorney General's office for your state's requirements. You can't beat a written estimate for security.

Most shops will quote a flat-rate price for your work. Using a manual that averages the time it takes for each job, they will quote and charge you a set price rather than the clockrate or actual time it takes the mechanic to perform that procedure at a given hourly rate. If you have any questions about the flat-rate price, ask to see the manual. If the price differs from that in the manual, you have a right to know why. Just as the best waiter can make a mistake in a bill, so can the best service writer or mechanic. Why not double check as you would for any other bill?

Once you have established a relationship with a mechanic you trust, you may be satisfied with a verbal estimate or even a ballpark guesstimate. You should always have an idea of how much a repair is going to cost before the work is done.

The more expensive a repair is likely to be, the more important an estimate is. If you're having the oil changed or a headlamp replaced, the rule of thumb "Always get a written estimate" may be overly cautious. A verbal estimate should suffice. If you're having your engine rebuilt, a written estimate could protect you from an economic nightmare.

If a shop refuses and says they can't give you any kind of estimate until they pull the engine or transmission apart, consider taking your car elsewhere. (This strategy of "take it out and tell you later" may, in fact, even be against the law in your state.) They may not be able to tell you what is wrong with the system until it is opened up, nevertheless, at a minimum, get an estimate in writing on the cost to disassemble, diagnose, and reassemble. Always find out what the maximum charge to you could be.

JOHNSTON CHEVROLET, INC.

3425 ALEMEDA DRIVE
SAN CARLOS, NEW MEXICO 87506
(505) 303-9786

NAME Mary Nelson			CUST. NO. 19252		R.O. DATE 7/23/87	MILEAGE 59125	TIME REC. 8:43	TIME PROM. 2:00pm
ADDDRESS 5705 S. Deleware Drive			ADVISOR 1361	RESIDENCE PHONE 303-6654	BUSINESS PHONE 345-6483			
CITY, STATE Santa Fe, NM			ZIP CODE 87501	V/E # 747564	DEL. DATE 10/2/84	DEL. MILEAGE 1		
YR. 84	MAKE CHEV	MODEL CAVA?WGN	COLOR BRN	LICENSE *&%BV	VEHICLE I.D. 1G1AD35P2G727315			

LABOR RATE IS BASED ON AN AVERAGE OF $36.00 PER FLAT RATE HOUR

ESTIMATE OF NEED REPAIRS   LABOR RECORD

QUANT.	PART NO.	PRICE	EXTENTION	EMP.NO.	COST	ELAPSED TIME	TIME CLOCK
	Pickup Coil	$45	/1978503				OFF
	Module	$60	/1979109				ON
1.8	Labor	$65		170			OFF
	Rotor	$7					ON
	Cap	$18	/1978497				OFF
	Plug Wires	$50					ON
	Plugs	$10		113			OFF
.7	Labor	$28					ON
	Air Filter	$12					OFF
.6	EGR Valve	$66	/17110504				ON
	Labor	$22		100			OFF
1.0	Scope Check	$30					ON
.5	Adj Idle	$20		50			OFF
							ON
							OFF
							ON
							OFF
							ON
				$433.00			
	TOTALS			TOTALS			

Whether you get a written or verbal estimate, or leave it all up to your mechanic's judgment, you should at least make sure you both agree on a few points. One is that if the estimate is to be exceeded by a certain amount or percentage (10 percent is a good rule of thumb), you must be notified and give your approval before the work is done. Leave a telephone number where you can be contacted and be there! Or agree on a time that you will call the mechanic to find out how things are going.

The same recommendation applies if while your car is in the shop additional or unrelated problems are found; insist on being notified for approval. If the additional repair is expensive and you're told that without it the car is dangerous to drive, be especially suspicious, unless this is a mechanic you trust implicitly. Remember you can always have the car towed to another shop. Never let yourself be intimidated or pressured into a repair job you feel uncertain about. Get a second opinion, even if it means the additional cost of a tow.

If you believe the estimate is high, are suspicious of the need for the repair, or simply want to compare prices, a second opinion makes sense. It isn't always necessary to take the car to another shop, although you may want to, especially if the car is still driveable. Instead, you may be able to get a second opinion or compare a price over the telephone. First, talk to the shop and make sure you are quite clear about what the problem is, exactly what needs to be done to fix it, and how much it will cost. Write down all the information. Second, call another mechanic or shop and ask what they charge to do the same repair. Be sure to give them the make, model, and year of your car first. You can ask for a guesstimate rather than a firm estimate if you are only interested in double-checking. Or you could explain the symptoms, the diagnosis, and the estimate, then ask the second shop for its opinion on the appropriateness of the diagnosis and cost.

Don't be afraid to use up some of their time. Service is their business and, besides, you may wind up taking the car to them.

Does the shop guarantee its work in writing? A common practice is to guarantee work for 90 days or 4,000 miles, whichever comes first.

How to Pick Up Your Car after It Has Been Repaired

Allow yourself 20 minutes or more when you pick up your newly repaired car from the shop. You will need at least this much time to discuss the repair with your mechanic, go over the bill, and test drive the car. If you pick up your car one minute before the shop closes and 15 minutes before you're due at your boss's house for dinner and then discover en route that the problem you just paid for is still not fixed, you could find yourself talking to a mechanic the next day who insists that the problem is a new one and intends to charge you accordingly. So arrive early whenever possible.

If there are any questions remaining about what work was done, or not done, speak to the person with whom you dealt with when you brought the car in for service. A good mechanic or service writer should be willing to take the extra 10 or 15 minutes to explain thoroughly, in plain English, the nature of the problem, what repairs were made or parts replaced, and how these steps related to your car's symptoms.

Ask for clarification on anything you don't understand no matter how simple or complicated it may seem. Your questions should be answered to your satisfaction. Listen carefully to the explanations and if you don't understand them, be specific about exactly what it is you do not understand. There are no dumb questions. It is your right as a consumer to be informed in a meaningful way. Ask to be shown (or drawn) a picture if words are failing. Keep getting more and more specific until you are comfortable with your level of understanding.

If all you receive are grunts and monosyllabic responses from two legs sticking out from under someone else's car, the relationship will be less than mutually satisfying. It's also important to remember that if you have the

attitude that any mechanic will cheat you given half a
chance, you may get a defensive reaction rather than an
informative response. Let the mechanic know that you're
interested in gathering information, not evidence.

Old Parts, New Parts

Don't be afraid to ask for your old parts back (in a plastic
bag for cleanliness, of course), but do so in advance. If you
are having a part completely replaced, however, your
mechanic may want to send the old part back to the factory to receive a rebate, called a "core charge." (Sorry, this
is not a savings that is passed on to the consumer.) The factory, in turn, will restore the old part to a nearly new condition and resell it as a rebuilt part. You may wish to pur-
chase a rebuilt part as a replacement. Rebuilt parts will
save about 40 percent; however, to guarantee quality,
make sure they are "factory" rebuilt or at least come with
a written warranty. You can still ask to see the old part
even if you can't keep it.

Remember that in asking to see the old part you could
actually be shown someone else's old part, but at least
you'll be making it more awkward for a dishonest
mechanic to rip you off.

The Bill

The bill should be legible and understandable. A bill that
is covered with smudged fingerprints and parts numbers
without descriptions is not acceptable. Go over each item
of the bill and make sure you are clear on how each one
relates to the symptoms your car was displaying or to the
routine service as seen in your owner's manual that you
requested. You should understand what was done and why.
Be specific.

Test Drive

Now you are ready to test drive your car. If you are not
completely satisfied that the problem has been corrected,
take your car back to the shop immediately and get a written acknowledgment from the shop manager that the

problem will be corrected and when. Stand on your two feet, open up your upper body, be firm, be clear, and be specific about what is not right. Remember, you don't have to be disagreeable to disagree.

What to Do When You "Can't Get No Satisfaction"

Keep accurate records, including all receipts and records of calls and letters and the name of the person with whom you speak, their title, and what their response is in each and every instance. Date every piece of pertinent material, including each repair record. Make sure the symptom, not the possible solution, is clearly stated on each repair order. For example, if the car cuts out completely, make sure the repair order says this clearly. Do not settle for the repair order to show a fuel problem. You will need written verification of the actual symptom that you are trying to have fixed.

Give them a chance to correct the error or oversight; honest mistakes do happen. If the problem is not corrected to your satisfaction, you may need to file a complaint, but first try the following measures.

Talk only to the owner or service manager from this point on. Be assertive, not aggressive. Assert your right as a consumer to have repairs done correctly.

If you do not get any satisfaction, pay for the cost of a written diagnosis from an independent mechanic. Do not, however, have the work done if the car is still under warranty.

Pay with a check or credit card whenever possible, but carefully read the entire invoice for evidence of a mechanic's lien. This leftover legality allows a shop to impound your car if you have signed the invoice and then deny payment for services rendered. If the state you live in honors mechanic's liens (and most still do), you are better off paying for the service and fighting for recovery later.

Send the Better Business Bureau a copy of a letter stating the problem. Contact the Consumer Protection Agency (often a division of the attorney general's office). Ask them to refer you to any local complaint handling panels. Get as much information as possible about how the panel works, what kind of problems they handle, who handles them, how they are handled (whether by written or oral arguments), within what period of time they make their decisions, and whether they are binding on you and/or the other party.

Notify newspapers, radio and television consumer advocates, and private consumer groups. Be certain you send a copy of your letter to the repair shop.

If you are not satisfied with the results of the complaint panel, you may wish to take your claim to small claims court. You will not need a lawyer, but be certain your claim falls within the limits of the court. Contact the consumer affairs office of the state attorney general's office for claim filing details.

What to Do When You Can't Get No Satisfaction and Your Car Is Still Under Warranty

As with a car that is not under warranty, talk only to the service manager or owner, and have a copy of your warranty on hand. If you do not get a satisfactory response, contact the manufacturer's district or zone representative (their name and telephone number should be listed in your owner's manual). Ask them for any service bulletin that might have relevant technical information for your car. Document the details of the problem and ask the representative to meet with you to discuss them.

If you are still unsatisfied, take your case to a local complaint handling panel or arbitration program of which the manufacturer of your car is a member. Arbitration programs are forums within which both the consumer and the dealer/manufacturer get an opportunity to state their side of the disagreement. These may be industry-run or state-run; the latter may require a filing fee. Depending on the car's warranty documentation, there may or may not be a choice as to which one you elect to use. The jurisdiction of arbitration programs varies.

Check your warranty documents for details. If you must go to arbitration, get all the advice and information available by contacting the consumer affairs office of the state attorney general's office: how the procedure is conducted, who is on the panel, how the case is heard (whether by written or oral arguments), how long before a decision must be rendered, and whether you must accept the findings of the panel. Usually decisions are binding on the manufacturer but not on the consumer. The most important part of these proceedings is that you follow the rules of the arbitration board to the letter, and that your case is well documented.

Lemon Laws

To protect consumers from manufacturers defects in new vehicles which are so serious that they result in the loss or reduction of the vehicle's use, value, and/or safety, most states have passed lemon laws. These laws further prescribe methods for compensation in the recovery of the cost of repairs and related expenses and even, in some cases, the replacement of the vehicle or refund of its value.

The specific requirements for asserting your rights under the lemon laws vary from state to state. To find out what your state's laws are contact your attorney general's office. The coverage time may be as brief as one year or as long as two years from the date of ownership or written warranty period. An authorized facility must have unsuccessfully attempted to make repairs for the same or different problem (this depends on how the state law is written) a predetermined number of times, or the car must be out of service and in the shop for a specific number of days during the coverage time. The dealer or manufacturer must be correctly notified of the problem and given the opportunity to fix it. This may mean a certified return receipt letter to the dealer, the manufacturer's customer relations office, and the local district or zone representative. Arbitration is the standard forum for resolution. It is not necessary for your state to have a lemon law for you to participate in arbitration.

If your problem is safety related, call the National Highway Safety Administration's toll-free number, 1-800-424-9393. They can give you information about safety standards, regulations, recalls, and references to other governmental agencies that can assist you in problem solving.

Glossary

Air conditioning condenser—a device that cools Freon, causing it to give up heat.

Air filter—a filter, usually of pleated folds of paper, designed to catch dust and dirt.

Alignment—see Wheel alignment.

Alternator—a motor that produces current.

Amperes (amps)—a measurement of electricity's strength or intensity.

Antilock brakes—high-performance, electronically controlled brakes that help to prevent lock-up.

Atom—the smallest division of an element.

Battery—a device that stores and generates electricity.

Ball joints—connecting devices that permit movement between two separate parts.

Bearings—devices that distribute and support weight while reducing friction.

Beads—thin strips of metal wound together into a narrow ring that provides a tire with an airtight grip on the wheel.

Bias-belted tires—tires that are constructed in such a way that the plies meet each other on the diagonal and are reinforced with strips of metal or fiberglass.

Bias-ply tires—tires that are constructed in such a way that the materials meet each other on the diagonal.

Bonding—a gluing process.

Boots—protective devices, usually rubber, that cover a part or a place where two parts meet.

Brake linings—heat-resistant friction materials that line the moving parts (shoes) of drum brakes.

Brake shoes—crescent-shaped pieces of metal that are lined
with heat-resistant friction materials.
Bushing—a metal or rubber liner that reduces wear between
two metal parts by acting as a cushion.

Caliper—a metal fist with one or two fingers (pistons) that force
disc brake pads against the rotor, causing it to slow or stop
turning.
Camshaft—a round metal bar with metal bumps, or lobes,
called cams which regulates the opening and closing of the
engine's valves.
Capacitor—see Condenser.
Carburetor—a device that combines air and fuel and distributes this mixture to the cylinders.
Catalytic converter—an emission control component containing chemically treated items that turn carbon monoxide
and hydrocarbons into such harmless substances as water
and carbon dioxide.
Choke—a door or plate located on top of the carburetor which
closes when it is cold, forcing more gasoline into the air/fuel
mixture.
Circuit—a complete pathway for electricity.
Clutch—a device that connects and disconnects the wheels
from the engine.
Coil—a booster or magnifier of electrical current.
Coil springs—suspension components that compress and
extend in response to irregularities in the road surface.
Combustion—the burning of the air/fuel mixture.
Compression—the squeezing or compressing of the air/fuel
mixture into a fraction of its former space.
Compression ratio—a numerical comparison of the size of a cyl-
inder from when the piston is at its lowest point of travel to
its highest point of travel, expressed in a ratio such as 12:1.
Compressor—a machine that compresses gas.
Computer—an electronic brain or microprocessor that receives
information from sensors and determines optimal driving
conditions.
Condenser—a tiny sponge that absorbs excess current.
Conductors—materials that transmit electricity.
Connecting rod—the metal piece that connects the piston to the
crankshaft.
Constant velocity joint (CV joint)—the connecting point at
which a driving and driven shaft meet.
Coolant—a solution of water and ethylene glycol that draws
heat away from the engine.

Coolant reservoir—a translucent container that serves as an overflow for coolant when it expands.

Core charge—the rebate received by a shop for returning a used part for a rebuilt part.

Crankshaft—the round metal bar to which the pistons are attached.

Current—the movement of electrons.

Cylinders—hollow tubes cut into the engine block that house the pistons.

Diaphragm—a thin disc, the vibrations of which convert electric signals to acoustical signals.

Differential—a specialized transmission that allows a car's outside wheels to travel farther and faster than the inside wheels.

Disc brakes— a type of brake that uses a caliper and kidney-shaped brake pads lined with friction material to stop a car.

Distributor—the ignition component that distributes voltage to the spark plugs.

Driveability— a term that refers to a variety of performance problems that cannot be readily diagnosed or easily fixed.

Dry gas—an alcohol additive that helps prevent gas line freeze-up.

Drum Brakes—a type of brakes that use a metal canister and two crescent-shaped shoes to which linings are glued (bonded) or nailed (riveted) to stop a car.

Electrolyte—a solution of water and sulfuric acid that when activated causes the opposite charges of the different plate metals to react chemically.

Emission controls—devices that reduce pollutants or chemically change them into harmless substances.

Engine analyzer—a testing device used to diagnose engine performance problems.

Exhaust gas emissions analyzer—a testing device used to determine the presence of exhaust gases in the radiator.

Exhaust manifold—a set of cast iron pipes attached to the engine which route burned gases away from the combustion chambers into the atmosphere.

Exhaust system—a series of metal components that are welded together to route burned gases away from the engine and into the atmosphere.

Evaporator—an air conditioning component consisting of a series of coils that absorb heat.

Fading—gradual loss of effectiveness as a result of heavy use.

Feed-back carburetors—carburetors assisted by an external computer.

Four-wheel drive—a power train that transfers power to all four wheels.

Front-wheel drive—a power train that transfers power to the car's front wheels.

Four-wheel steering—a system in which the rear wheels steer as well as the front.

Fuel filter—the filter that is responsible for cleaning gasoline by catching dirt and foreign particles before they reach the working parts of the carburetor or fuel injectors.

Fuel injection—the modern-day equivalent of the carburetor. This computerized blender combines air and fuel.

Fuel injector—the device that sprays the air/fuel in a fuel injection system.

Fuel pump—the mechanism that draws gasoline from the fuel tank to the engine. It may be mechanically or electrically powered.

Fuses—the thinner wires encased in plastic or glass which guard the electrical system by melting, thus breaking circuits in response to surges of excess electricity.

Fusible links—lighter pieces of wire placed in a circuit which melt in response to surges of electricity. Similar to fuses but without a protective casing.

Gas line freeze-up—ice crystals that form in gasoline during cold weather which starve the engine of fuel by clogging the openings of the carburetor or fuel injector nozzles.

Gas-powered shock absorbers—shock absorbers that use a nitrogen charge to pressurize the fluid in the tubes.

Gears—round metal-toothed wheels used to produce turning power.

Gear ratio—the number of turns a driving gear makes compared to the driven gear.

Hydraulic—any system that operates by fluid under pressure.

Hydrometer—a device that measures the amount of sulfuric acid remaining in the battery's electrolyte solution.

Hydroplaning—a condition that causes a tire to lose traction when a layer of water is formed between the tire and the road surface.

Ignition—the system that produces the spark for the air/fuel mixture.

Impeller—the portion of the torque converter that is attached to the flywheel.

Incandescence—to become white with heat or to glow.

Independent suspension—a suspension system in which each wheel responds independently to changes in the surface of the road.

Insulators—materials that offer substantial resistance to the flow of electricity.

Intercooler—a device used in combination with turbochargers and superchargers which cools air, making it less dense.

Input shaft—the shaft leading from the engine to the transmission.

Journal—the part of a shaft that turns on a bearing.

Knocking—a sound heard as a metallic rattling, pinging, clicking, or knocking which is the result of improper combustion.

Leaf springs—suspension components that consist of uneven strips of metal that absorb the motion of the car's wheels as they flatten and unflatten.

Lean mixture—an air/fuel mixture in which less fuel is used in proportion to air.

Lever—a metal bar or handle.

Linkage—any system of rods and levers.

Load tester—a piece of testing equipment that simulates electrical load or need.

Lube job—a procedure that removes old grease and replaces it with clean grease.

Lubricant—any liquid or solid that coats an object with a thin film to provide a slippery cushion to prevent friction.

MacPherson strut—a suspension component that combines the spring and shock absorber into one unit.

Master cylinder—a reservoir for brake fluid which is divided into two separate sections, each section activating a different pair of brakes.

Molecule—the smallest division of a compound.

Muffler—a member of the exhaust system, this device absorbs much of the sound that combustion creates by routing sound waves through its hollow chambers.

Multigrade oil—oil that contains additives that give it the qualities of more than one grade of oil.

Multiport fuel injection—an air/fuel mixer and distributor that mixes and delivers an individualized ideal diet of air and fuel for each cylinder through fuel injectors.

Multivalve engine—an engine that is equipped with additional intake and/or exhaust valves that permit the engine to breathe and burn more air and fuel.

Octane—the rating of a gasoline's ability to resist knocking.

Ohms—a measurement of resistance to the flow of current.

Oil—a liquid, usually petroleum-based but possibly synthetic, that acts as a lubricant, a cleanser, and a cooling agent.

Oil filter—a pleated paper device where dirt and contaminants, the natural by-products of combustion, are caught and stored.

Oil gallery—an enclosed passageway with smaller passageways leading from it through which oil moves to lubricate vital engine parts.

Open—any condition that interrupts the flow of current.

Output shaft—the shaft leading from the transmission to the wheels.

Oxygen sensor—a device that monitors the richness or leaness of the fuel mixture.

Pinging—a light metallic rattling or clicking similar to marbles or ball bearings hitting together.

Planetary gears—gear sets that provide changes in gear ratios in automatic transmissions.

Plies—pieces of material attached to the bead of the tire. The material and the angle at which they meet each other determines the tire's construction category.

Points—a component of traditional ignition systems, these metal arms open and close causing the coil to become saturated with electricity.

Power steering—the assistance provided by hydraulic fluid that can be added to both traditional and rack and pinion steering.

Rack and pinion—a lightweight steering system consisting of a pinion gear and a long rack with teeth.

Radial tire—a tire with lines (cords) that develop symmetrically from a central point, like the spokes of a wheel. The construction materials meet each other at right angles and are reinforced with strips of steel.

Radiator—a device that stores and circulates coolant.

Rings—thin round metal hoops that surround the pistons.

Rebuilt—a part that has been restored to a nearly new condition and resold as a replacement.

Receiver—a dryer that separates and removes moisture in the air conditioning system.

Relays—backup safety switches that are used on circuits where strong current develops.

Rotor—a metal disc connected to the wheel.

Scheduled service—a list of maintenance procedures that manufacturers recommend be performed every so many weeks, months, years, or miles.

Sending unit—a device that monitors volume or temperature.

Sensor—a device that receives and feeds back data.

Shock absorber—a sealed suspension component system filled with fluid that contributes to the smoothness or harshness of the ride.

Sludge—the unburned deposits that form as a result of combustion.

Solenoid—an electromagnetic coil that acts as a switch.

Spark plug—a metal and ceramic device that produces a spark.

Specific gravity reading—the measurement of a battery's state of charge.

Springs—suspension components that compress and extend to absorb the motion of the wheels on irregular ground.

Starter—an electrical motor that starts the engine running by turning the crankshaft.

Stator—a vaned wheel that causes fluid to turn in one direction only.

Steering—the system of rods, levers, and gears that controls the direction of a car.

Supercharger—a device that is driven by a belt that forces engines to breathe more air.

Suspension—the system that controls the car's up-and-down motion.

Synchronizers—devices, found in manual transmissions, with teeth (dogs) that slide in and out of the various gear combinations, locking them into place.

Switch—a piece of metal suspended between two pieces of wire that serves as a gate for the electrical current, turning current off and on.

Synthetics oils—oils made from a nonpetroleum base.

Thermostat—a one-way heat-sensitive door that permits the flow of coolant to the radiator once a predetermined temperature is reached.

Throttle body fuel injection—a mixing system that sprays a common measure of air/fuel to the cylinders.

Throw-out bearing—a clutch component resembling a metal doughnut that disengages the clutch.

Tie rod ends—the connecting joints of the steering system.

Torque—measured turning power.

Torque converter—the mechanism that connects and disconnects the engine from the automatic transmission.

Torsion bar—a spring that absorbs road motion by means of a bar that twists and turns.

Traction—adhesive friction.

Tread—the grooved face of an automobile tire.

Tread depth indicator—a device that when inserted into various grooves in a tire measures tread depth.

Transmission—the gear mechanism that links the power of the engine to the wheels.

Tune-up—the routine replacement of spark plugs, filters, and other air, fuel, and ignition-related parts, plus a precise series of tests and adjustments performed every 7,000 to 30,000 miles to regain maximum engine performance.

Turbine—a machine with blades which spins fluids around.

Turbocharger—a device that uses some of the excess heat generated by the engine to force more air into the engine.

U-joints—the metal connecting points that join and facilitate movement between the driving and driven shafts.

Vapor—a fine spray or mist.

Vapor Lock—a condition that occurs when gasoline turns from a liquid to a vapor resulting in an engine that is starved for fuel.

Valves—one-way doors that regulate the flow of the air/fuel mixture into and out of the cylinders.

Valve guides—metal shells or sleeves within which the valves move up and down.

Valve train—components that help the valves open and close including springs, rocker arms, pushrods, and tappets.

Variable load shock absorber—a shock absorber that mechanically or electronically responds differently to various weights carried in the car.

Viscosity—an oil's ability to flow at different temperatures.

Viscosity index improvers—additives that give an oil the qualities of more than one grade of oil.

Voltage—the force or pressure of electricity.

Voltage regulator—a device that regulates the flow of the alternator's current.

Wattage—the amount of power produced by an electrical current, as measured in thousands of watts or kilowatts and kilowatt-hours.

Water jacket—the sleeve of copper-lined passageways that surrounds the cylinders through which coolant circulates.

Water pump—a device that circulates coolant.

Wear bar indicator—a patch of smooth rubber inserted into the tread of a tire indicating it is time to replace the tires.

Wheel alignment—the adjustment or position of the angle of suspension components to affect a predetermined angle for the car's wheels to meet the road.

Wheel balancing—a procedure in which small pieces of metal, called weights, are attached to the lighter spots on a wheel to make it turn evenly.

Wheel bearings—devices that resemble metal doughnuts with many ball bearings inside which distribute the weight and turning force of a shaft.

Wheel cylinder—a device that pushes out against drum brake linings, causing the wheel to slow or stop.

Wind-up—the strain that results on the power train when both axles of a standard part-time four-wheel-drive vehicle are locked together and forced to turn at the same speed on dry pavement.

Index